ALPHA
PREDATOR

How To Be Victorious

Over Life's Ultimate Adversary

and

What To Do When You're Not!

Steven R. Taylor

A Blood Washed Khaki Publication

ISBN: 978-0-9887261-3-0 Hardback
ISBN: 978-0-9887261-0-9 Paperback
ISBN: 978-0-9887261-1-6 Kindle

A Blood Washed Khaki Publication
123 W. Grand Street, Borger Texas 79007
www.bloodwashedkhaki.com

Cover photo by Steve Evans

DEDICATION

To Mom and Dad, whose liberating love and support always generated longing to return but never guilt for having gone.

Geoff,

From my heart and the heart of Africa!

1 Peter 5: 8-11

ACKNOWLEDGEMENTS

I wish to express my deepest gratitude and profound admiration for the following people who in an amazingly broad diversity of ways have inspired and participated in the production of this book:

Judy Hart – Retired English Professor, and one of the most deeply committed Christians I've ever known – for her editorial assistance and literary encouragement.

Steve Evans – Photographer, adventurer, and long-time friend – for the outstanding cover photo of a lion mask, depicting the Alpha Predator.

Buck DeVries – Lion Hunter, conservationist, deep personal friend – for being the embodiment of everything I love about wild Africa and for his and his wife Rita's support of our ministry over the years.

Matt Cox - for his technological assistance and computer skills - without whose assistance the formatting of this book would have been impossible. Faithful, loyal, courageous, trustworthy - indispensable friend.

The International Mission Board of the Southern Baptist Convention – for making it possible for us to spend those years in Africa, and for being the best and most complete support base missionaries could ever hope for.

The Tonga people of the Zambezi River Valley - because of their lives, my life will never be the same. Thank you for including me and for interrupting Tonga history so I could get on board and become a part of it.

First Baptist Church of Borger, Texas, as well as other faithful churches with whom I've been associated – for supporting and making possible each year a return to the Zambezi River Valley for an annual short-term mission trip with a wonderful group of volunteers, and for allowing time and opportunity for the preparation and delivery of Biblical messages from God's Word.

My children, who all love the Lord, missions, adventure, and the African people – for being living testimonies of the fact that one of the greatest blessings of life is when the children you raise, as adults become your very best friends.

And finally, but certainly not in the least, *Shirley* – my faithful wife – to whom I owe 1,000 nights for the loneliness she endured while I was away camping in the bush, and 10,000 soft pillows for the discomforts she experienced when she went along with me. I owe her a million ice cubes for the deprivations she withstood while I was following my dreams, and I owe her my very own life for all those times when she never stopped believing in me, never ceased leaving a light on in the window, and never gave up searching or praying when everyone else thought I might be helplessly lost in lion country. I haven't forgotten who the real hero in this story is.

Table of Contents

ALPHA PREDATOR

al·pha pred·a·tor (al′fə prĕd′ə-tər, -tôr) – An Alpha Predator; also known as an Apex Predator, Super Predator, or Top Level Predator is one that has no predators of its own, residing, as it does, at the top of the food chain.

FIRST ENCOUNTER

Powder blue breath vapor swirled pungently in the moonlight as the huge lion lifted his head and roared. Dry twisted seedpods fell from high in the thorn trees as the intense voice of the monarch shook the grass and foliage. "Is this the sound of unfiltered ferocity?" I did not know. But, when the force of that felt volume hit my listening ears, my understanding of the sound of impending death was forever changed.

Steven R. Taylor
First encounter with wild African lions
Zimbabwe, Africa – 1981

FOREWORD

Sounds of the night began to rise in an increasingly raucous chorus. The pleasant aroma of cook fires in the distance drifted through the gnarled branches of the nearby Acacias and Msasas. Breathing slowly and deeply, Steve and I continued our visit, inhaling the atmosphere of Africa that always seemed so pronounced in this garden on the outskirts of Bulawayo, Zimbabwe.

Earlier that afternoon, I had driven Steve to see this interesting and out-of-the-way garden near our house. As we walked its trails we began to talk seriously about what had brought us, and our families, to Zimbabwe. We spoke of total abandonment to the will of God, the testing of faith, and our eager desire to see God move mightily among people whose lives were being severely tested by a new government rapidly disintegrating under the leadership of a seemingly demonic despot.

Before leaving that garden, Steve and I knelt in prayer, committing ourselves afresh to God. It was a rich moment, a moment to savor, a moment neither of us wanted to forget. Seeking somehow to keep that moment fresh in our memories, we found a rock that we broke into two pieces. We each vowed to keep our half of the rock as a reminder of that surrender to Christ's Lordship over our lives. Today, almost thirty years later, my piece of that rock remains in the center drawer of my desk in our home in Oklahoma.

While the two pieces of that rock have changed very little, each of us, and our families have changed a great deal, and for the better, I believe. Our separate pilgrimages have driven us to experience God's grace in ways neither of us would have ever imagined. The one constant for us both has been the Rock, Jesus, to Whom we have had to run, upon Whom we have had to lean, and in Whom we have had to hide from the "predator" time and again.

Alpha Predator is a remarkable book authored by a remarkable man, my friend, Steve Taylor. Steve's writing is colorful, riveting, and filled with "weather." His knowledge of Africa is expansive and remarkably intriguing. But this is a book hammered out on the anvil of Steve's own experience. He writes with a rare transparency, gifted exposition, and moving application.

At this very moment *you* are being hunted down by a cunning and clever predator; a powerful predator for which you alone are no match. But you do not have to face this predator alone! You can . . . . Well, you will just have to let Steve tell his story.

Tom Elliff
President, International Mission Board
Southern Baptist Convention

INTRODUCTION The Tragic Death Of A Young Man In Africa

"Ah, Mufundisi, they only found small pieces of his body scattered through the bush!"

Mapulanga wasn't smiling as he related the story, and Mapulanga had the greatest smile I've ever seen on the face of an African. We were standing together under the shade of a lemon tree. I had been watching Mapulanga's melancholy expressions all morning, and I had seen the signs of sadness etched across his face, so I had not yet spoken. The African way is not to rush in the midst of emotion. Still, I genuinely wanted to know what had happened, so when I caught his glance, I asked him with my eyes. He began to tell the story.

"It was there." he said, as he shook his head, lifting his chin and pointing with pursed lips to a place just across from our house on the Zambezi River. *"It was there where we see the light shining every night from those light globes powered by the big generator at that safari camp near Matusadona."*

I reached up and pulled a lemon from the tree, stuck my thumb into it and peeled it back as I took a seat on a nearby rock. I used the peeling as a pointer to motion toward another rock as I offered Mapulanga a seat. He took his seat and spoke softly once again, *"This is the story they tell. It seems a young man had come out from England on holiday with a group of his friends. They were taking pictures of the animals there in the bush. When darkness came, they sat around the fire talking until they were tired. When the young man went to his bed where he had pitched his tent far from the others, he left the tent door open. When the night became quiet and still, the lions came looking for food. Everyone was awakened by the screaming. The lions took that young man from his tent and they ate him right there while the others were listening. Ah, Mufundisi, they only found small pieces of his body scattered through the bush!"*

Though brief and straight to the point – so typical of the way the BaTonga people narrate a story – Mapulanga's words left a haunting picture hanging in my mind. I found myself thinking often of the episode over the next several days. Having many times seen prides of hunting lions violently ravage their prey in the remote area of the Zambezi River Valley where my family and I were living as missionaries at the time, I could readily visualize how terrible the final moments of the young man's life must have been. When during the following week I finally made my way into town, the newspaper reports only verified what I had already begun to assume had taken place.

"I heard a horrendous yell!" The newspaper quoted David Boyle, a fellow photographic tourist, as he described the horrible death of the nineteen-year-old British student whose life-long dream it had been to spend a year in Africa. *"I didn't know if it was human or animal. But it was long*

and loud, and it was suddenly cut off, followed by the prolonged sound of growling." [1]

I stood reading the description of how in the pre-dawn darkness of that ominous August night in 1999, David Pleydell-Bouverie was attacked and savaged by a pride of ten to twelve lions. According to the reports, he died only a minute or two after the attack began. But by that time, much of his body had been shredded and eaten by lions in the deep bush of the Matusadona wilderness area in Northwestern Zimbabwe. When the sun came up the next morning, local game rangers found parts of his dismembered body strewn through the bush up to twenty yards from his tent.

Unaware, We Had Been Watching from the Far Side of the River

On the night of the attack my family and I had been sitting on the front veranda of our home in Siavonga, Zambia, looking across the river, as we often did, gazing at the lights of Zimbabwe dancing on the surface of the water. We often entertained ourselves in the evening by imagining what life must be like for those people enjoying the adventure of falling in love with Africa for the first time in the safari camps there on the other side.

The red-orange light was the first to fade as the guides and tourists grew tired and let the camp fires burn low. Soon the brighter white lights also faded as the generator motors were switched off in the safari camps; their dying mechanical coughs sending alien sounds of false security ringing through the forests as the tourists made their way safely to their tents. Nobody ever dreamed that night the young Englishman would fail to heed the warning to keep his tent tightly zipped. Nor did they expect him to pitch his tent at a distance dangerously far from the main group. But neither did they expect him to be dead within the space of just a couple of hours of time from when they walked away from the fire, wishing one another a pleasant sleep.

The young man had spent such a wonderful day of game-viewing, sight-seeing, and photography with his friends. But life in the African bush is always uncertain and tenuous at best. The lions were roaming that night, looking for an easy meal, and young David Pleydell-Bouverie was selected as the target.

For the next several weeks, I found myself dwelling on the events surrounding the young man's death. After all, I personally had camped many times in the same general area – alone and unprotected except for the companionship of the faithful African people. The more I investigated the details of this tragic event, the more I discovered that David Pleydell-Bouverie had died for all the wrong reasons. Avoidable circumstances, mistakes, and human error all contributed to his untimely death.

A Terrible Reminder of the Words of Peter

The young man's death was a terrible and graphic real-life reminder of the words of Peter in 1 Peter 5:8-11. In these verses, Peter writes a warning about a horrendous Alpha Predator who is roaming the earth *"like a roaring lion"* seeking to destroy the lives, and annihilate the testimonies of God's people. *"Be sober! Be on the alert! Your adversary the Devil is prowling around like a roaring lion, looking for anyone he can devour. Resist him, firm in the faith, knowing that the same sufferings are being experienced by your brothers in the world. Now the God of all grace, who called you to His eternal glory in Christ Jesus, will personally restore, establish, strengthen and support you after you have suffered a little. To Him be the dominion, forever. Amen.*"

Of all the followers of Christ living during New Testament times, Peter was uniquely qualified to issue this warning and impart this promise. He had personally fallen victim to the Alpha Predator's attack one night when he had repeatedly denied the Lord, even after he had convinced himself that he never would. He had known the dreadful pain this Adversary is capable of inspiring. He had become fully aware of how subjective failure can open the door to a full-scale attack by this awesome Pillager.

Perhaps that pain is the thing that makes it easy for so many of us to identify with Peter. He writes as a fellow struggler who has been through a very personal and violent encounter with the Alpha Predator. That encounter had resulted in defeat and failure, leaving him reeling in spiritual downfall and remorse. Had it not been for the grace-drenched initiative taken by the Lord to bring about Peter's restoration, he would have gone to his grave as a broken and defeated man.

The Anatomy of Restoration

This book is a book about defeat, failure, and restoration in the believer's life. In it I invite you to take an honest look at how to be victorious over life's ultimate adversary and what to do when you're not victorious. I really wish I could say I am writing *only* from a hypothetical perspective. I would like to be able to say that none of the references to failure and defeat found here have any basis in the historic reality of *my* life. But, honestly I have to tell you, that fantasy is not the case. I know what it is to fail and I know what it is to be defeated. I know what it is to be discouraged and to be knocked out of the race. I know what it is to have such a terrifyingly close face-to-face confrontation with the Alpha Predator that I have seen the reflection of myself deep in the orbs of those giant unblinking amber eyes. And gazing at that reflection, I know what it is to be ashamed – ashamed for not seeing in that reflection a likeness of the Lord, but rather the misshapen caricature of a wounded and broken man – a dishonorable contortion of the person He created me to be – a defeated and fallen facsimile of the intention of God for my life.

But thankfully, I also know what it is to be the unworthy recipient of a restorative work of grace – undeserved and unattainable apart from an acknowledgement of my helplessness, frailty, and absolute dependence on God. I know what it is to find release in the refuge of an honest heart before the Father, to learn the vernacular of confession and contrition, the one true dialect of deliverance that communicates the way back home.

Thus I know what it is to enter a period of self-imposed seclusion, to find a lonely place where I could concentrate on re-establishing the vital connection of my heart with the only One in Whom I have ever found liberation. I know what it is to make enforced solitude and obligatory isolation the daily occupation of my life. I know what it is to sit day after day in the silent places of the night, and in the quiet places of the day, in obscurity and separateness with an open Bible on my knees, waiting and listening for the Voice of the Holy One in the pages of His Word.

I know what it is to find in those pages a God-designed soul-friend, a faithful *anamchara** of sorts with whom I could identify and who could instruct me through a passage in his first letter to an understanding of the anatomy of restoration. **(Anamchara* is a beautiful old Gaelic word and literally means *"friend of the soul."* It was originally used in the ancient Celtic churches to describe someone who shared another's jail cell as an encouraging companion and to whom one confessed, sharing the most confidential aspects of his life. Ray Simpson defined an *anamchara* as *"A soul friend who helps a person re-weave the scattered elements of his life into a new wholeness.")*[2] This picturesque passage from the Apostle Peter's writings (1 Peter 5:8-11) serves as the Scriptural basis for this book and as an outline of God's process of restoration in the believer's life. It is the description of the restoration of a real life of a real believer.

This restoration experience is too significant for me not to share! The reason for this is simple – sooner or later the Alpha Predator launches his attack on the life of every believer. Even if the believer doesn't fail in the midst of the attack, he often fails in his successive response to it. I have a feeling there are many people out there who need a word of hope from the personal experience of an actual life. They desperately need to hear the truth that according to God's Word, restoration after failure and defeat is not only conceivable and authentic, it is intended, expected, and made possible by God.

So, if today you find yourself in a fight for your life with life's ultimate Adversary, or if you have already been conquered in the fight and find yourself thinking because of your defeat, life for you has come to an end and your relationship with your Lord can never be what it was before, then this book is for you! While the Bible makes it clear there is an "Alpha Predator" who is real, cunning, and ferocious – a marauder who destroys, plunders and devours – the Bible also makes it clear there is One Who is both Alpha and Omega, infinitely greater than any Accuser, and the final word is always His. He holds the keys to forgiveness, restoration, and the rebuilding of your life! *"To Him be the dominion forever! Amen."*

PART ONE: How to be Victorious

TAYLOR

CHAPTER 1 Victory Through Vigilance

"Be sober! Be on the alert! (1 Peter 5:8a)

The remote bush of Zimbabwe and the lack of convenient access to vehicle repair shops give a whole new meaning to the concept of a "shade tree mechanic." A person quickly learns he must be innovative when it comes to vehicle repair and upkeep. Making fan belts out of his wife's panty hose and keeping his battery fresh with pennies on the posts and aspirin tablets in the cells is something every bush missionary must learn.

One of the greatest challenges faced by a bush missionary regarding vehicle upkeep comes simply from the extreme pounding the vehicle must endure in the course of day-to-day operation. The rough roads and paths of those extremely remote locations constantly hammer the vehicle's frame and make changing shocks almost as routine as changing oil. Also, because of the pounding, battery cables and terminal connections wear out over time.

That disaster in the making was the case on one particular day in 1992. We were living in Kamativi, Zimbabwe, at the time, and guests had come to visit from the states. They were anxious to see the wildlife of

11

Zimbabwe. For at least a couple of weeks prior to the arrival of our guests, I had been having problems sufficiently securing my battery cables. They simply would not remain continually attached while traveling on the rough roads of Zimbabwe, and I just had not had the time to travel the six hours to the city required to replace them.

A beautiful spring afternoon greeted us when we headed out for Hwange National Park, where I assured our guests we would see plenty of wild animals before dark. We had chosen a great day for game viewing. With our children enclosed in the camper on the back of the Land Cruiser, our guests were in the back seat of its stretched cab. The day was truly delightful. The Cruiser was running great and we darted around Hwange locating, enjoying, and photographing various species of God's creation. We must have seen 500 elephants that afternoon, and kudu and impala were so plentiful by late afternoon we no longer even slowed down when we passed them by. The giraffes towered above us on both sides of the road, and jackals, zebra, and wildebeests were scattered on every horizon. We saw ostrich and eagles, hornbills and lilac breasted rollers, secretary birds and crimson breasted shrikes. We came across Cape buffalo in a thick mopane forests and sable and roan antelope feeding in the tall grass.

The one thing our guests really most wanted to see, however, had eluded us all day. No lion! What is an African game drive without lions? Desperately trying to be a good host, I stopped at waterhole after waterhole (in Zimbabwe called a "pan"), yet everywhere we looked, there were still no lions. I could tell by the looks on their faces, our friends were more than just a little disappointed.

As the sun began to sink and in an effort to bring joy to our guests, I turned down a particularly primitive overgrown road full of Kalahari sand traps and washes. There were no other recent tracks from safari vehicles, and acacia thorns scraped the sides of the Cruiser indicating it had been a long time since anyone else had passed that way. After traveling through the thorn jess and mopane thickets for several kilometers, the two little parallel sand paths finally opened up at a place called Sinanga Pan. As if on cue, there at the pan was a large pride of lions lying in the midst of tall taupe-colored ant hills. There must have been a dozen of them. Because I wanted our guests to have "the full African experience," I pulled the truck as close to the lions as I dared and switched off the engine. After all, I assumed we would be perfectly safe as long as we stayed inside the vehicle.

From an endless list of game viewing experiences in Africa, this was the best experience with lions I have ever had. Not more than thirty yards away from the truck were twenty-four amber eyes gazing intently at us as we studied their teeth and whiskers through the high-powered lenses of our binoculars and repeatedly photographed their fly-dowsed faces in all their bloodstained detail. *Yes, a near perfect afternoon!*

Darkness was setting in by that time, and we were required by law to be out of the park and back to the main gate no later than sundown. With the main gate, still being twenty miles away, I announced to the group it was time to go. After a few, "*Oh wow! That was great!*" type comments, I reached for the steering column and turned the ignition key. Nothing! Absolutely no sound! And that "sound of silence" when the engine refuses to respond to the ignition deep in the African bush is an awful sound - especially when time is running out. When no one knows where you are and you are in a place where it's not likely that anyone will stumble across you for a long time either; when you are responsible for your wife, your guests and your children; when your engine won't start and the lions are glaring at you while planning their evening meal, you might honestly describe the situation as being "in a real spot." Not wanting to cause panic, I looked into the moon-shaped eyes of our guests and politely smiled. At the same time, my mind raced for a course of action.

"Ah, yes! That is it! The battery cable must have come off once again."

Under normal circumstances, that would have been no problem. I would have simply gotten out of the vehicle, opened the hood, re-attached the cable and we would have been on our way. Twenty-four hungry eyes were watching our every move now, and when the old male licked his lips, I thought for a moment I saw him raise his eyebrow and smile.

Sometimes it seems my wife Shirley has a knack for asking the obvious. With her usual calm and quiet voice she said, *"What are you going to do?"*

I said, *"Somebody is going to have to get out and re-attach the battery cable."*

She said, *"Hurry back!"*

So, after a full round of stressing that everyone must carefully watch the lions and shout if anyone should detect even the slightest movement, gently and as quietly as possible, I opened the door to the driver's side of the truck. Unfortunately for me, my move didn't go un-noticed. Ears and eyes on the furry gang immediately came to attention. After swallowing hard, I looked back at Shirley and said once again, *"Watch them closely."* Then I took one step out. Immediately I stopped and looked back one more time, and at the risk of sounding redundant, whispered, *"Watch them closely!"*

As I eased toward the front of the truck, I'm sure our crowd thought I was trying to do my best impersonation of a layer of Toyota clear coat. For some reason, however, I just couldn't get close enough to the truck body to ever really feel comfortable. The moment I dreaded most was when I would have to turn my back on the pride and open the hood of the vehicle in order to re-attach the cable. At that point, for a few seconds, my back would be turned toward the lions, and for that moment the opened hood would at the same time obscure my view of Shirley's eyes as she watched the lions for movement. Needless to say, I didn't plan to "dillydally" with my re-attachment move.

With my hand on the safety lever which holds the hood in place, I felt one of those "heart in my throat" kind of feelings roll over me, and I quickly, yet smoothly as possible lifted the lid. *"Whew!"* It was only a loose cable after all, and I wasted no time re-attaching it. I then quickly sealed it down by using my fist as a hammer, and in one hurried move I closed the hood and looked for Shirley's eyes.

The most difficult part of the whole affair was trying not to run back to the truck door and thus trigger a charge from the lions. At that instant I recalled the advice of an old professional lion hunter friend who once said, *"When moving around lions, one can never let fear dictate the pace!"* As carefully as possible, tighter than a water-soaked chamois, I slid back down the fender of the truck and practically leaped inside the door. Incredible relief swept across me when I was inside once again! I learned a very important lesson that day, too. The lesson is this: if you are going to get outside in lion country, you better always be watching!

The First Principle of Victory

This coincides precisely with how Peter begins his great "Alpha Predator" passage in 1 Peter 5:8-11. *"Be sober! Be on the alert!"* When you live and walk in lion country, you are in no place to be either unaware of, or oblivious to, what is going on around you. You better be constantly watching! As anyone who has ever failed can tell you, avoidance of failure is always better than restoration. Therefore these two Biblical commands as related by the Apostle Peter, make up the first principle of victory when it comes to dealing with an Alpha Predator attack.

The Meaning of Peter's Words

"Be sober! Be on the alert!" – very precise, yet very meaningful words! The word translated *"be sober"* is *"nepho,"* and in the New Testament *"nepho"* is always used in a figurative sense. Literally it means, *"be free from every form of mental and spiritual intoxication."* The verb form Peter uses is an aorist imperative and that verb form

always calls for urgent action. Therefore, "*nepho*" conveys the idea of freedom from excitability, impulsiveness, and volatility. It refers to a posture of composure especially under stress. It means taking heed of what is happening in one's environment and thus pursuing a course of action with calm and steady aim.

In this sense, Peter is directing us toward serenity and balance in the midst of stressful situations. This is the precise opposite of mental uncertainty. It is a picture of the essential steadiness and poise of a person who knows what he believes, and thus faces life with a sense of moral alertness.

On the other hand, the word translated "*be on the alert*," is "*gregoreuo*" and it refers to a constant state of readiness and vigilance. A disciplined awareness of one's surroundings and an unceasing attentiveness to even the tiniest movement in the bush are essential components for moving safely through lion country. Lions are just so unbelievably fast and can complete a successful charge in mere seconds – sometimes faster than a man can even react. A professional hunter in Africa once told me if a hunter has his rifle slung over his shoulder when he meets a lion in open country, and the lion charges from a distance of fifty feet, there is no need for the man to try to bring his rifle down for a shot. A full-tilt charge from an African lion is so fast that the man will never have time to get his rifle down from his shoulder before the lion is on him.

Among the ancient Greeks "*gregoreuo*" was used to describe people carefully crossing a river while stepping on slippery stones. It describes the value they placed on the necessity of paying careful attention to their every step. If they were less than exactingly cautious, they would end up in the water.[1] This is the alert posture Peter is stressing.

Peter uniquely understood the importance of this. He, no doubt, had played over and over again in his mind the memory of that time in Gethsemane when he and his fellow disciples had slept instead of watching with Christ. Christ had come to His disciples and warned them that they should stay awake and pray lest they enter into temptation. (Matthew 26:41) *"Gregoreuo,"* in this context, literally means, *"Stay awake! And do it with a sense of urgency."*

An illustration of the critical consequences of failing in this necessity is found in the Lord's warning to one of the churches in the Book of Revelation. In New Testament times, the city of Sardis was considered to be a natural citadel in the ancient world and thought by many to be incapable of being captured. But, in fact, there were several times when the city was captured. However, each time this happened it was determined that the city fell because of the self-confidence and the consequent failure of a city guard to stay alert and to be watchful. Therefore, when our Lord warned the church of Sardis regarding their tendency toward spiritual slumber, He used the exact same word that Peter uses in 1 Peter 5:8. *"Be alert and strengthen what remains . . . but if you are not alert, I will come like a thief and you will have no idea at what hour I will come against you"* (Revelation 3: 2-3, emphasis mine).

Distraction Is the Method of Satan

Each year under the name of Rock Cry Expeditions, I return to the Zambezi River Valley with a group of intrepid and risk-taking volunteers for a short-term mission trip. We travel to the deep bush regions of Northern Zimbabwe to engage the BaTonga people with a message of hope and salvation through Jesus Christ. For a little more than two weeks we journey in rugged four-wheel-drive vehicles, eat simple meals, and sleep hanging in expedition style hammocks near the villages of some of the most beautiful people on the face of the earth. Their simple lifestyles, honesty, and deep commitment to hospitality make our stay among them one of the most enjoyable experiences imaginable.

However, in order to reach them, an excursion of 8,000 miles each way is required, and in the course of that journey we travel through some of the most theft-ridden cities of the world. That being the case, among the many subjects I cover with the team during our pre-expedition orientation time is the subject of personal theft potential and specifically, the danger of pickpockets. I stress repeatedly with the team members the importance of not being distracted in crowded airports, restaurants, and public places as we travel along the way. The importance of keeping one's wits about oneself and one's surroundings cannot be overstressed when it comes to global travel.

Though there appear to be many different kinds of pickpockets and con men that a person may encounter along the way, they all use a common technique – distraction.

There is a tendency for human beings to focus on only one thing at a time. The pickpocket knows this and takes advantage of this fact by getting his victim to focus on anything other than his money or valuables. These distractions can be very elaborate, ranging from staged fights by accomplices, to the entertaining antics of cute children. Sometimes they even "accidentally" spray a foreign substance like ketchup or mustard on an individual, and then pretend to help him wipe it of his clothes – whatever it takes to distract the person from his belongings.

Sometimes a pickpocket will take advantage of the kindness of the victim and will pretend to accidentally drop something so the person targeted will stop and bend down to help him. When that occurs, an accomplice comes up from behind and snatches the wallet or valuables of the person who has been good enough to stop and assist the original perp.

Some pickpockets are so clever that they will distract a victim from his money by actually bringing his attention to it. *"How is that possible?"* This is how it goes down. One member of the team will shout in a crowded place, *"Somebody just stole my wallet!"* When they hear that, most people will immediately reach for the pocket where their wallet or valuables are stored. This makes the pickpocket's job much easier. Now he knows exactly where to look simply by watching the hands of those people right around him.[2]

Distraction is the key, and the reason I am sharing this with you is that this is the same strategy that the Alpha Predator employs. Satan will often seduce people with distractions while he proceeds to ravage their lives. *"Be sober! Be alert!"* Be constantly watching!

Do you remember the "hidden camera" television series *Candid Camera*? It debuted in August of 1948 and was seen periodically until 2004. Created and produced by

Allen Funt, the show was based on concealed cameras filming ordinary people being faced with extraordinary situations. Sometimes the response of those people made them come across as quite foolish and usually very humorous. When the gag was up, the person being filmed was usually "let go" with the show's catch phrase, "*Smile, you're on* <u>*Candid Camera*</u>!" Most often everyone laughed and a good time was had by all.

On one particular show, the point of the ploy was to demonstrate how easily some people can be distracted. An actor bent down on all fours and pretended to be looking for something. As he persisted, pedestrians began to notice and soon many were also on the ground looking for whatever the actor had lost. The gag came when the actor carefully and quietly withdrew himself and left a number of people still on their knees intensely involved in the search. They continued to search even though the original "searcher" had left the scene.[3]

Satan is aware there is in each one of us an inclination toward distraction. That is why we are warned repeatedly in Scripture to maintain a posture of spiritual alertness. Peter lists this as the first and primary principle when it comes to dealing with the schemes of the Alpha Predator. In defense against his attack, we should post a watchman at the doorway of our minds and the gate of our eyes and ears to guard our hearts from any devious, seductive intruder that might attempt an assault.

Years ago someone said, "Our last day is a secret in order that every day may be watched." We should be careful to live every day as if it is our last day, cautiously guarding our lives with a spiritual alertness that prevents an intruder from distracting us from the way of the Lord. We must be sober and always be watching!

Jesus' Parable Illustrates This Truth

During His final week of ministry, Jesus communicated a parable to four of his closest disciples stressing the importance of this continuing state of alertness. One day, He was seated privately with Peter, Andrew, James and John, and in response to a question from them, He shared this parable. *"It is like a man on a journey, who left his house, gave authority to his slaves, gave each one his work, and commanded the doorkeeper to be alert. Therefore be alert, since you don't know when the master is coming – whether in the evening or at midnight or at the crowing of the rooster or early in the morning. Otherwise, he might come suddenly and find you sleeping. And what I say to you, I say to everyone: Be alert!"* (Mark 13:34-37)

The Greek scholar Marvin Vincent made this comment on Jesus' emphasis on a wide awake, alert doorkeeper. "In the temple, during the night, the captain of the temple made his rounds, and the guards had to rise at his approach and salute him in a particular manner. Any guard (doorkeeper) found asleep on duty was beaten, or his garments were set on fire."[4]

This simply underscores the importance of Peter's admonition concerning spiritual alertness. In fact, this is the first principle in a successful and victorious encounter with the Evil One. "Be sober! Be on the alert!"

A Faithful Watchman

In the introduction of this book, I referred to one of the most wonderful friends I had the privilege of knowing during our days on the mission field – Mapulanga. He was a trusted African companion and a reliable colleague. He was so dependable that I actually assigned to him the responsibility of watching over our youngest daughter McKelvey while she played in our yard in order to keep her safe from the hippos and crocodiles that sometimes wandered there. He was also the gatekeeper for our home. Mapulanga was a faithful man.

Every time I left our house for an extended period of time, the very last thing I would say to Mapulanga was, *"Muli mucengeta!"* *"You are the guard!"* He knew by that I was putting him in charge of keeping my house and my belongings safe. He also knew when I said that to him I was holding him responsible. Sometimes after many days away I would come back home at an odd hour or unexpected day. It did my heart good to discover again and again that Mapulanga was faithfully guarding the place. He was devotedly keeping watch.

I recall coming home on one particular night at a very inconvenient hour. I had been delayed in the bush by a punctured tire or some other mechanical problem, and the night was well into the early morning hours before I managed to get back to town.

I drove slowly into the sleeping village of Siavonga that night, desperately attempting silence, long overdue from my expected and "respectable" time of arrival. I saw no one moving in the darkness, and a unique sense of intrusion inhabited the inactivity of those early hours. The cool African night air still held traces of suspended blue-white smoke from the previous day's cooking fires. A tinge of embarrassment rolled over me as the vehicle noise seemed to shout, *"Wake up everybody! Mufundisi is home."* I felt somewhat like a teenager tip-toeing on a creaking wooden floor, trying to successfully and quietly negotiate his father's curfew, every sound at that hour being magnified as if it were the only sound in the world. The rhythmic metallic clicking of the smooth running Toyota diesel engine reverberated from every flat wall I passed, with the cadence of an ill-timed drum being beaten by a rude percussionist suffering from insomnia. The tedium of the repetitive tread roar from the cruiser's all-terrain tires by this time was beginning to grate on my nerves, as well. So, it came as a welcomed relief when, at last, I brought the vehicle to a stop at the gate. I had to shake my head to clear the volume of the rumble from my hearing. The wind and the tire roar and the engine noise had by that time become like the mesmerizing monotony of an aboriginal didgeridoo. I urgently needed to change the tune.

The gate was located a few feet off the road at the top of the hill. From there I would descend the flagstone driveway to our house situated on a flat place down the hill nearby the river. As I tried to quietly ease the vehicle closer to the gate, the sand which had accumulated on the brakes began to squeak with the same shrill endless sound of the fruit bats that hang in the eucalyptus trees in Harare. I felt an exceptional solitude and wondered if anyone else in all of Siavonga was awake that night to hear that sound. But then in the light of the headlights I saw the flash of

Mapulanga's smile as he walked briskly up the hill toward the gate. He had been sitting in his usual place on the rock under the lemon tree keeping watch over my house and my family. When I saw him, it was obvious from his alert disposition he had been waiting and watching in the darkness. But, he had not been asleep. He was wide awake!

After an obligatory polite greeting, I spoke in ChiTonga with gratitude and a deep sense of admiration, *"Muli Mucengeta - wamasimpe."* *"You are the guard – the real one."* Mapulanga just smiled and said, *"Eyi! Ndime mucengeta wamasimpe. Teewakandijana nkindiledepe."* *"Yes! I am the guard – the real one. You did not find me sleeping."*

"Be sober! Be on the alert!" The first principle of spiritual victory when you face a challenge from the Alpha Predator is spiritual alertness. *"Satan is prowling around like a roaring lion looking for anyone he can devour."* He is out to destroy your life. If you're going to live in lion country, then <u>you better stay awake.</u> <u>You better be alert.</u> <u>You better always be watching!</u> Victory comes through vigilance. That is the first principle of success when Satan attacks.

TAYLOR

CHAPTER 2 If You Run, You're Ruined

"Resist him, firm in the faith" (1 Peter 5:9a)

"The most terrifying of all African big game narratives!"[1] – that is how Geoffrey Haresnape, Emeritus Professor at the University of Cape Town, describes the telling of the events that took place one August night in 1903 when African lions attacked South African game ranger Harry Wolhuter. His is without doubt one of the most popular and one of the most well-known of all African lion stories. I personally have heard the story told by professional hunters and conservationists around as many as a dozen African campfires.

The story goes that Wolhuter, a relatively new game ranger at the time, had recently been sent out to hunt down and shoot a man-eating lion that had killed an African woman and her child. Returning after dark on patrol, he was riding on horseback in the Sabi Game Reserve area of what is now the Kruger National Park in South Africa. Following him at a distance was his staff, bringing along with them his camping supplies and equipment on the backs of pack donkeys. In addition to his staff, the pack donkeys, and the horse, there were several good hunting dogs in the procession. One particular dog named Bull followed closely behind Wolhuter when he decided to ride on ahead of the rest of the group.

The steady rhythmic sound of the constant tempo of his horse plodding along the dusty path was the perfect accompaniment for the joy of his solitude. The unsullied scent of the deep wilderness was a gratifying indulgence as each breath filled his lungs with the pleasure of a transparent washing. Such is the night in Africa. But this environmental lullaby crooned no warning of what would happen next. The serenade of the bush was about to make one of its typical yet radical crescendo shifts.

Except for the company of the dog, Wolhuter was completely alone when the first lion attacked his mount, knocking him out of the saddle in the process. Tumbling from the saddle, he fell right into the jaws of a second lion that immediately sunk its teeth into Wolhuter's right shoulder and promptly began to drag him off through the bush. Meanwhile, the first lion chased the horse as he raced off through the darkness of the night, with "*Bull*," in turn, close behind in hot pursuit.

Wolhuter was now being dragged on his back between the legs of the lion. He later related he was so close to the cat's muzzle that he could smell traces of blood and meat on the lion's breath. Yet, in spite of his very perilous position at that moment, he recalled he had a sheathed knife strapped to his belt on his right side. Painfully contorting himself, he was finally able to reach behind his back and grasp the knife with his left hand. He could only use his left arm since most of his right shoulder was in the lion's mouth. Yet, he realized he must do something rather quickly. He had already begun to imagine how horrific the experience might become if the lion actually began to eat him before he was dead.

Carefully bringing the knife around his back and across the front of the lion's chest to the left side of the lion's rib cage, Wolhuter made two quick, yet strong back-handed jabs in an attempt to stab the lion's heart. The knife penetrated deeply and the big cat lifted his head and gave a loud roar. As he did so, Wolhuter struck upward with the knife, and judging from the amount of blood that spewed out all over him, he assumed he must have hit the lion's jugular vein. The commencement of this crimson shower caused the lion to react dramatically and it released him and quickly disappeared into the darkness.

Wolhuter then stood up and screamed like a wild man as he chased after the wounded lion in its retreat. However, when his senses began to return and his adrenaline began to wear off, he realized the precarious vulnerability of his pursuit and rallying his remaining strength, he climbed a tree. Sitting unsteadily on a limb in the tree he began to feel faint and used his belt to strap himself to a branch in order to keep himself from falling out. It was there in the tree his staff later found him strapped to its branches, and after several days of demanding travel they at last brought him to medical treatment. Even though after many days in the hospital he recovered fully from the initial attack, his wounds and subsequent bouts with infection left him severely scarred. Sadly, his health was weakened from the attack for the rest of his life.

Perhaps the reason for the popularity of Wolhuter's story, and certainly the reason why he survived the attack, is because he fought back with everything at his disposal. Wolhuter's response to the attack of this big cat is a reminder to us of what Peter says our response should be when attacked by the great Alpha Predator, Satan. Peter begins verse 9 of 1 Peter 5 by saying *"Resist him, firm in the faith . . . ."* He says this is where we must begin our defense if we are to withstand an attack by the Alpha Predator.

The Second Great Principle of Victory

In Chapter One we saw that avoidance is the ideal response when it comes to a satanic attack. Through vigilance and acute awareness of Satan's ploys, we can avoid many of his attacks and save ourselves so much trouble and heartache. However, even in spite of our most watchful vigilance there comes a time in the life of every believer when Satan launches an all-out assault. When that time comes, Peter says *"Resist him, firm in the faith . . . ."* *Fight back with everything you've got and refuse to run*! This is the second great principle of victory when it comes to an attack from the Alpha Predator.

If a man is attacked by a lion in the African bush and if he has no weapon for protection, he stands very little chance of surviving the attack. The lion is so strong and his assault is so powerful that without a weapon the unarmed man is almost certain to become a fatal statistic. However, if you ever find yourself in that situation, you need to be mentally prepared. Do you know what you should do to give yourself the best chance of survival? Many people certainly do not!

For example, many people assume you should run away as quickly as possible. After all, that is the most natural response. But running is actually the absolute worst thing you can possibly do. Running shows you are weak. It reveals you as potential prey. And it stimulates a lion's natural instinct to chase. The lion is an "alpha predator" and he knows you are there in his environment long before you realize he is there. You cannot outrun him, outmaneuver him, or easily evade him. If he is determined to attack you, he will. So lesson number one is to resist the urge to run!

Cowardice never wins in a battle against a lion; only courage prevails. If you are attacked, fight back. Never succumb or try to roll into a ball. That may sometimes work with bears in America, but never with lions in Africa. Instead, look the lion in the eyes. Never turn your back. And, if you are attacked from the back, try to reposition yourself to meet the cat face to face as quickly as possible. Under no circumstances should you ever fall to the ground and roll into a fetal position. If you do, the lion will just think you are nothing but small prey and will begin eating you quicker.

That's why, if you can, it is always best to carry a weapon when you are walking alone in lion country. If you can't outrun him, you better find a way to resist him. Experts will tell you that you should use anything you can find to fight back – and weapons you find at random in the bush are not always conventional ones. So, find a stick or a rock, throw sand in his eyes; even bite his nose. But if you can't avoid the attack and have no other weapon, these makeshift tools are your only defense. One thing is sure – if you run you're ruined! That will do nothing more than trigger an immediate charge.[2]

In one of his classic books on hunting dangerous African game, professional hunter Peter Capstick tells about a time when a lion attacked his faithful gun bearer Silent, while he slept in a temporary grass hut in a hunting camp in Zambia. Having had experience with lions in the past, Silent knew he must fight back as the lion continued to maul him through the wall of the hut. But in the confusion of the attack and in the darkness of the African night, Silent was unable to locate his spear. Feeling around with his hands on the dirt floor, he desperately searched for the blade and shaft without success. Then, in desperation to find a weapon, he grasped something cool, smooth, and hard. He snatched the object up and with a full, un-opened bottle of Coca-Cola, he began to beat the lion mercilessly across his snout. He continued to do this with passion and desperation until at last the lion turned and ran off into the bush. Capstick concludes his story by saying, "*It had to be the only recorded instance of a man driving off a marauding lion with a Coke bottle!*"[3] But all this proves my point. If you are ever attacked by a lion and you have no weapon, use whatever you can find and make a weapon from that. It is your only hope for survival. Whatever it takes, "*resist . . . stand firm.*"

"Resist him"

The word translated *"resist"* in this passage is the Greek word *"anthistemi"* from *"anti"* meaning, *"against,"* and *"histemi"* meaning *"to stand."* *"To resist"* therefore, literally means *"to stand against"* or *"set oneself against."* This, by the way, is where we get our English word, *"antihistamine,"* used in cold and flu medicines to treat runny noses and sneezing, or itching from a rash. The *antihistamine* works against those things, and thus it *"resists"* or *"stands against"* their influence and affliction on the body of the one so suffering.

To *"resist"* the Alpha Predator is to take a posture of opposing him in every way possible. It pictures a face-to-face confrontation and a decision to oppose him with firm determination. Originally the word *"resist"* referred to an army arranging itself in a battle against an enemy force. The Christian is at war in this world, and he must build fortifications against the Alpha Predator himself.[4] This tactic is exactly the way the Apostle Paul uses this word *"resist"* with reference to spiritual warfare in Ephesians 6:13, *"Therefore, take up the full armor of God, so that you will be able to <u>resist</u> in the evil day, and having done everything, to stand firm."* [Emphasis mine]

One of the most important principles often presented and repeatedly given in Scripture for successful Christian living is that the believer is to flee from various kinds of evil. In 1 Corinthians 6:18, we are told to *"flee immorality."* In 1 Corinthians 10:14, we are told to *"flee from idolatry."* 1 Timothy 6:11 tells us to *"flee from [the love of money.]"* 2 Timothy 2:22 tells us to *"flee from youthful lusts.*" But instructively, we search throughout the Scriptures and never find a single verse where we are told to "*flee from*" the devil. Instead we are commanded flatly to "*resist him*," and "*he will flee*" from us. We are not to run!

Just like a lion's chasing instinct is triggered by a prey animal that runs away, the instinct of the Alpha Predator to destroy you is triggered if you show any sign of cowardice, whatsoever. "*Resist him!*" This is a command from God Himself, and whatever God commands, He enables us to do. The most dangerous thing you can ever do is to "cave in" to the Alpha Predator's intimidation.

There is a great example of this found in the Old Testament book of Daniel, chapter three. There we find the story of three young Hebrew men: Hananiah, Mishael, and Azariah. More often we refer to them by their Babylonian names: Shadrach, Meshach, and Abednigo. The story of their lives is a true story that gives us an Old Testament illustration of a New Testament principle regarding spiritual battle with the Alpha Predator. We find they were under extreme pressure to forsake their loyalty to God and exchange it for religious loyalty to the Babylonian king Nebuchadnezzar. The king had declared that everyone in the entire kingdom was to bow down to and worship a ninety-foot tall, pure gold image of himself. But these three young men would not do it. They surprised the king, and he was determined to make them suffer greatly for it. But still, these three young men would not budge. They "*resisted*" him regardless of what he tried to force them to do. He had the idea that "*everyone has their price.*" But they were determined to remain faithful to God, regardless.

So, they "*defied*" the king. In a similar way, the Bible tells us that we are to "*resist*" the evil one.

At this point in Daniel's story, the three young Hebrew men uttered some of the greatest words of faith to be found in God's Word. "*If we are thrown into the blazing furnace, the God we serve is able to save us from it . . . but even if He does not rescue us, we want you to know, O King, that we will not serve your gods or worship the image of gold that you have set up*" (17 - 18). That is a stance of determined resistance. They took their "*stand against*" the king. And that is the proper stance of our lives, as well, when we encounter the Alpha Predator.

"*. . . firm in the faith*"

The word, translated "*firm*" is the Greek word, "*stereos*" and it means "*stable, steadfast, or solid like a foundation.*" In the physical sense this word describes something as firm, hard, solid, and dense as a stone. In the figurative sense it is used to describe food adults eat – solid rather than liquid or mush like infants eat. That describes the nature of the faith with which we should stand in defiance of Satan. Taking a stand against the Alpha Predator is no child's game.

Stereophonic Faith

During my sophomore year in high school, I turned sixteen on March 10, 1967. The following summer I worked all summer long hauling hay and caring for a stable of Tennessee Walking Horses in order to save enough money for my first car. My first car was a 1955 Buick. It was a green and white straight shift, with a big-block 8 cylinder engine, the new high compression ratio, and 236 horsepower. I was so proud of that car! Because of the increase in engine displacement and horsepower in Buick models for that year, the 55 Buick is considered by some to be one of the first true muscle cars. It would run and it would run fast. But what it had as an advantage in horsepower, it lacked terribly in the sound system. The radio was basic – and I mean basic with a capital "B." In fact the radio was a monophonic sound producer, and it sounded somewhat like a hand-held transistor radio. You would think I could have expected much more. After all, I paid all of $150.00 for the car! Anyway, the engine was respectable and the car handled nicely, but the radio was lousy.

So, I'll never forget the day when after working all of the summer as a stable boy baby-sitting half ton superstar show ponies, I made my way to the local Western Auto Store and purchased a brand new true "stereophonic" 8-track tape player and speakers, and had it all installed in my Buick.

(For those of you, "post-1980's folks" who may be reading this – Stereo 8 was created in 1964 by a consortium led by <u>Bill Lear</u> of <u>Lear Jet</u> Corporation, along with <u>Ampex</u>, Ford Motor Company, <u>General Motors</u>, <u>Motorola</u> and <u>RCA Victor Records</u>. It was basically an endless loop magnetic tape cartridge, slightly less sophisticated than CD's or iPods, but our closest 1960's "reasonable" likeness.)[5]

Wow, what a sound! Compared to the monophonic speaker "sounds" of the original equipment, the new "stereo" was "*groovy*." *Uh um, I mean "wonderful."* I used to drive down the road listening to Bob Dylan and Simon and Garfunkel sing, saying to myself, "*Wow! That is a 'solid' sound.*" After all, it was "*stereo.*" And that is exactly what the word "*stereo*" means.

But long before there was "*8-track stereophonic sound*" in my Buick, there was "9th*-verse stereophonic faith*" in 1 Peter, chapter 5. And the stereophonic faith described there is a faith enabling the Christian to stand fearlessly and firm against "*the roaring lion.*" This solid faith describes personal confidence in God and His Word. That confidence comes from the fact that the basic nature of faith is confidence that things yet future and unseen will happen just as God has promised in His Word they will. Peter is saying if that is the nature of our faith, we will be enabled to stand firm, regardless. Personal confidence in God and His Word is the key to standing firm.

Our Lord Jesus gives us a clear example of this while dealing with the temptations of the evil one in the midst of His wilderness temptations. Every temptation was met with an appropriate passage from the Word of God. When we take our stand on the Word of God, we will be enabled by the Father to withstand the attacks of the Alpha Predator.

The Apostle John, writing to the church in his first epistle, said to the young men, "*I have written to you, young men, because you are strong and the Word of God abides in you, and you have overcome the evil one*" (2:14). As the believer feeds on God's Word and assimilates it into his life in obedience to God's truth, Satan is resisted. Faith based on a personal confidence in God and His Word is "stereophonic faith." It is solid and it is firm. That was the position of the three young Hebrew men mentioned earlier in Daniel, chapter three. And that's why they said, *"We're going to serve God regardless."*

Nebuchadnezzar's response to the "solid" faith of those three young men was fierce anger. In fact, as one of my former seminary professors used to say, *"He became wroth with a capital "R!"* So the king said, *"Turn up the heat! Make the furnace seven times hotter than usual."*

Do you realize that the heat and the size of the furnace that Satan tries to throw you into is a compliment to the quality of your faith? Once you really begin to take God seriously and really begin to take a stand for His truth, you'll find the devil saying, *"Turn up the heat! Turn up the heat!"* But that is what can be called *"the flattery of the furnace."* The hotter the furnace, the greater the compliment the Alpha Predator is making about the reality of your faith.

Early in our missionary days in Zimbabwe, I entered a remote village in one day and immediately from the other end of the village an old witch doctor began to curse me and maniacally laugh at me and criticize me to those who were standing around her. I had never seen or met her before, but from the moment I stepped into the edge of the village, she began to mock me and ridicule me as a missionary of Jesus Christ.

Years later I shared that experience with a mission study group in the states. Someone in the group asked, *"Did that not bother you? Did it not discourage you and frighten you to be spoken of with such mockery and derision by a witch doctor?"* But I answered, *"No! In fact, it was a great encouragement to me. I took it to be a compliment to my faith. If the evil one who abides in and controls her so completely recognizes the One Who abides in and owns me, the lines are clearly drawn. At least everyone in the whole situation immediately knew whose side each of us was on."*

I took the experience to be an affirmation of Christ's ownership of my life and my identification with Him in His suffering. It encouraged me to stand firmer and to risk more for His glory in that part of the world. Though each of us can know absolute verification of the authenticity of our salvation through the promises of God in His Word, it is added assurance when a servant of the evil one recognizes the One for Whom we stand and curses us because of that fact. That's the *"flattery of the furnace."* The hot fire is a clear sign Satan is taking you seriously because you have begun to take God seriously. That is simply the Alpha Predator's response to solid faith and the firm resistance of him with your life.

Does the Alpha Predator know you by name? Do the demons recognize you as a sold-out follower of Jesus Christ? It is a compliment to your faith when the resistance of your life becomes so well known to the inhabitants of hell that the evil one considers you a personal enemy.

There is a fascinating passage in Acts 19:11-16 that gives us insight regarding this truth. We read:

"God was performing extraordinary miracles by Paul's hands so that even facecloths or work aprons that had touched his skin were brought to the sick, and the diseases left them, and the evil spirits came out of them. Then some

of the itinerant Jewish exorcists attempted to pronounce the name of the Lord Jesus over those who had evil spirits, saying, 'I command you by the Jesus that Paul preaches!' Seven sons of Sceva, a Jewish chief priest, were doing this. The evil spirit answered them, 'I know Jesus, and I recognize Paul —but who are you?" Notice, the demon said, *"I know Jesus and I recognize Paul."* Leonard Ravenhill referring to Paul while commenting on this passage, describes him like this, *"Over this God-intoxicated man, hell suffered headaches."*[6] Is your reputation for always fighting back and refusing to run such that you are known by the spiritual forces of darkness? Are you known by the Alpha Predator as a *"firm resistance,"* *"solid-state"* servant of God? Are you famous in hell? Do the demons shudder at the mention of your name?

I love the way Dave Earley and Ben Gutierrez put it in their wonderful book, *Ministry Is.* They ask the question, *"What are you doing to insure that your face is on the walls of hell's Post Office? Do the demons talk about you as "Most Wanted!" "Most Feared!" "Approach carefully, considered armed and very dangerous?"*[7]

C. T. Studd once said, *"I pray that when I die, all hell will rejoice that I am no longer in the fight."*[8] Is your life making that kind of difference for the cause of Christ?

The second great principle of victory when attacked by the Alpha Predator is firm resistance. Fight back with everything you've got and refuse to run away!

ALPHA PREDATOR

This Is No Time for Running Away

During our mission years, living among the BaTonga people of the Zambezi River Valley in Zimbabwe, my family and I lived in a little village town called Kamativi. Our nearest "real" grocery store was six hours away through the bush in the city of Bulawayo. That being the case, if we wanted fresh meat without the inconvenience of a long trip, I had to go out and hunt it, shoot it, field-dress it, bring it home, and cut it up on our kitchen table – all this before Shirley turned it into a delicious meal for our family.

(By the way, Shirley makes some of the best Kudu Pizza in the whole world. You can look for Shirley's new book – *Fun and Famous Recipes for Kudu Pizza* – Coming soon. Only joking!)

Fortunately for us, our nearest European neighbors were generous Safari Operators who allowed me to come and hunt on their land whenever we needed fresh meat. So about every month or six weeks I would travel the short distance from our home to the Gwayi River Valley where I would dispatch a Kudu or Impala from our local supply of protein.

One particularly beautiful, sunny afternoon I asked my son Rye to go along with me on the hunt. Walking a short distance from the truck, we had been hunting only for a brief time when a big Kudu bull appeared from behind an ant hill and quickly made his way over a small rise before I could even manage a shot. (Kudu are often referred to by locals as the "*Grey Ghost*." The reason for this nickname is their uncanny ability to appear and disappear so rapidly in the Zimbabwe bush.) I looked at Rye, who was only

41

eleven years old at the time, and realized in order to be successful in bagging the Kudu I would likely need to go alone from that point. Then I began to plan my stalk.

I knew there were lions in the area, but felt sure there would be no danger as long as the sun was shining brightly and Rye kept still. I led him to a nearby *vlei* or "meadow" covered with long grass and told him to sit quietly and still. I would be going just over the hill to shoot the Kudu and I would be back in a matter of minutes. *"Whatever you do,"* I told him, *"don't leave this place until I return for you. I'll be back soon."*

When I got to the top of the hill, I looked toward the next horizon and as I did so, I caught a glimpse of the Kudu just as he went over the next rise. I thought about Rye sitting alone in the grass on the *vlei*, but since it wasn't far, I decided to proceed on with the stalk. When I topped out over the next rise, much to my surprise, the same thing happened again and I just caught a glance of the bull as he cleared the next horizon. This scene continued repeatedly until, at last, I was able to catch up with the Kudu, make my shot, and secure our family's dinner.

Unfortunately, more time had passed in the process of the stalk than I had imagined. Now the afternoon shadows of the forest and bush were growing rapidly and I knew I had to get back to Rye right away. I began to make my way back at a fast pace. When I came over the last hill separating us, I looked down on the *vlei,* and there in the middle of it was a little blonde head turning back and forth looking anxiously in every direction.

By this time, not only were the shadows of the evening growing, it was also getting cold. When the sun goes down in the African winter time, it gets amazingly cold compared to the warm African days. Now, I really felt badly about leaving him for so long!

When I finally reached him, I apologized. I said, *"I'm sorry son. That took much longer than I thought it would. I know I told you to sit here, but when I didn't come back after a little while, why didn't you just run to the truck. It wasn't that far away."* He looked up at me with trusting eyes that seemed to say he was surprised I would even ask that. Then he said, *"Dad, when you left, you told me you would be back for me soon. You told me to sit here in this field. You didn't tell me to run to the truck. So I didn't run. I stayed. I did what you told me to do."*

As believers we live in an inhospitable world, and Satan's attacks come at us from every side. Our world is cold and uncaring, and in the light of His promises to return quickly, it seems the Lord has been away for quite a long time. Some days I grow weary of the fight. Some days I would just like to run away. But when Jesus left, He left us with a mission to accomplish. He told us to stay faithfully in the field until He comes again and to stand toe to toe with the Alpha Predator. So we need to heed the words of Peter, *"Resist him, firm in the faith."* This is no time for running away. It is no time to be running to the truck. In fact, <u>if you run, you're ruined</u>. So fight back with everything you've got and refuse to run away!

TAYLOR

CHAPTER 3 Tribal Warfare

"knowing the same sufferings are being experienced by your brothers in the world." (1 Peter 5: 9b)

"Africa . . . One word, and every man who has ever imagined adventure conjures a dream."
– Mike Gaddis[1]

My growing up years were spent in the company of the legendary characters of Africa. As a child, Sunday afternoon television was reserved for Edgar Rice Burroughs' *Tarzan, the Ape Man.* As a teenager, rainy days and late nights were often spent peering over the shoulder of fictionalized "great white hunters" like Allan Quatermain, who lived out his escapades on the pages of H. Rider Haggard's *King Solomon's Mines.* By the time I was a young man in college, I had progressed to exploring the lives and adventures of the "real-life" heroes of Africa. During those years I read much about men like David Livingstone, Robert Moffat, Colonel John Henry Patterson, "Karamojo" W. D. M. Bell, and Frederick Courtney Selous. As far back as I can remember I have always had a fascination with the people, the wildlife, and the land of Africa.

Thus, people who knew me well were not surprised when in 1981 my life took a radical change of direction. For it was then in response to the call of God that my wife, my family and I pulled up the roots of our American way of life and moved to Zimbabwe, Africa, to become international missionaries.

So, for the past thirty-plus years, our lives have been bound up in one way or another with the lives of the people there. Up until the time of our departure for Africa, I had only experienced the exploits of the great champions of Africa in a second-hand fashion; now I have actually walked down some of the same game trails and bush paths where Livingstone, Selous, and others wandered.

All of those early pioneers are gone now. They were gone long before I ever set foot on the continent. But, I wish I could have known them personally. There are so many things I would have enjoyed discussing with them – so many things left unsaid and unanswered in those early books.

A Modern-Day Selous

While those early giants of African history have all departed now, there are still some personified vestiges of their kind, who, with the same independent spirit, have remained and thrived in that rugged land. One of the great privileges of my life is that I have had an opportunity to meet and know some of those legendary leftovers. One of those renowned relics is a man by the name of Buck De Vries. Buck De Vries is one of the most interesting men I have ever known. A retired lion hunter, conservationist, bush pioneer, and adventurer, all rolled into one, Buck De

Vries is a native white African of South African Afrikaner descent, and a personal friend of mine. Buck is like a walking encyclopedia of African bush knowledge. His experience with the flora and fauna of Zimbabwe is evident in every conversation. Much of what I have learned about the African bush veldt I learned from this man.

While my family and I were living and serving as missionaries in the Zambezi River Valley, Buck and his wife Rita were our nearest white neighbors. In those days, we visited with them often, and they have become some of our dearest friends. Each year when I return to Zimbabwe with a group of volunteers for a short term mission trip, I always stay in Buck and Rita's home for at least a couple of nights, and it is always a great joy to spend time visiting with them.

In 2002, as result of Zimbabwe's Land Acquisition Act, Buck and Rita were removed from their land and wildlife conservancy in the Gwayi River Valley and had to leave the place they had called home for more than forty years. A few months before this event took place, my family and I had to leave the Zambezi River Valley to return to America. Just before our departure, we spent a week with Buck and Rita in their home.

During that week Buck and I hunted together to secure his favorite breakfast fare – fresh Kudu liver. We also spent many afternoons just sitting quietly at the waterholes of the Dete Vlei, watching the amazing wildlife of that game-rich area. During that time, I recall seeing one of the largest herds of elephant I have ever seen in the course of all my years in Africa. It was a storybook ending to our wonderful years of residence in that marvelous country.

The Most Impressive Scene in Africa

Finally we came to the last afternoon before our departure. Once again, Buck and I found ourselves sitting quietly on the edge of the Dete Vlei. A slight breeze was blowing through the teak and mopane trees and once again it brought over me the rush of a familiar feeling which I can only describe as the *"atmosphere of freedom."* (If you have ever experienced that feeling on a late afternoon in Zimbabwe, you know what I mean.) But now, the time had come for my final farewell to the Zimbabwean bush.

As I looked in the direction of my illustrious companion and recognized his long time experience with the wild places and wild creatures of Africa, I couldn't keep myself from asking a question that had often been on my mind. *"Of all the striking places and scenes you have ever seen here in Africa – of all the experiences you have had, and all the days in the bush you have lived through, what would you say is the most stunning, the most awesome, the most impressive scene you have ever witnessed?"*

Honestly, I expected him to describe a scene involving the thundering hooves of some prey animals narrowly escaping the razor sharp claws of a team of predators. Or perhaps, I thought, he would describe a raging bush fire of gigantic proportions with a myriad assortment of animals running ahead of it to evade its fiery wrath. Or maybe I expected he might refer to the silhouette of a pair of giraffe feeding on the leaves of a thorny acacia tree, stately standing with necks crossed perfectly against the red-orange background of an exceptionally gorgeous sunset.

But what he was about to share was nothing like that. In fact, his answer took me completely by surprise.

I watched as his eyes narrowed across the vlei with the focus of a memory replayed often in his mind. A slight smile gathered beneath his roughed out mustache. He turned back to me, and in that moment I can't say whether the moisture in the corner of his eye was from sweat or a tear. But he finally spoke with the deep accent of his Afrikaans heritage. And as he spoke, his eyes somehow softened from the predatory gaze of the hunter he had been in the past, to the compassionate observation of the naturalist and conservationist he had become. *"No Steve, the most beautiful sight I ever saw in the African bush occurred right here in this vlei. It was when the herds of Impala were giving birth to their young. Do you realize when they start giving birth; the whole herd will all drop their young within an hour or so?"*

Reflecting on what Buck had just said, I could not help but be reminded of the words of our Creator God as He spoke to Job in Job 39:1-4, *"Do you know when mountain goats give birth? Have you watched the deer in labor? Can you count the months they are pregnant so you can know the time they give birth? They crouch down to give birth to their young; they deliver their newborn. Their offspring are healthy and grow up in the open field."*

This thought then came to my mind – *"When the impala are giving birth in the Dete Vlei, God is watching, too. Is something like this scene what He had in mind when the Bible repeatedly describes God's assessment of His creation in Genesis, chapter 1 as 'good . . . good . . . good . . . good . . . good . . . good . . . very good?"*

But I had to ask, *"Why do they do that? Why do they all give birth at one time?"*

"The lions!" He spoke quietly and he paused, nodding his head ever so slightly. I wondered whether he was affirming his own words or if the effort of the memory had somehow fatigued him. *"The only hope the fawns have for survival is their large numbers. Their security comes from the fact that they are no longer just individual impala babies scattered here and there. They are a whole herd – all at once and at one time."*

Obviously, I thought, the anti-predatory benefits of herding are apparent. There are a number of benefits to it. Herding provides increased sensory potential and dilution of risk. It provides greater physical defense, and increased predatory confusion. It also provides a reduced predator/prey ratio and an increased foraging/vigilance ratio. But regardless how we may describe the benefits of herding, it is a clear example of the principle of safety in numbers.

Brothers in a Brotherhood

Just like the impala babies, all coming into the hostile world at one time, we as believers need each other for support, encouragement, and defense. Peter endorses that concept when he writes, *"knowing the same sufferings are being experienced by your brothers in the world"* (1 Peter 5: 9b). The word he uses for *"brothers"* is a very meaningful word in the original language. The usual Greek word translated *"brother"* is *"adelphos."* Therefore the plural of that word, translated *"brothers"* is the Greek word *"adelphoi."* But the word Peter uses here goes beyond that.

His word is *"adelphoteti."* Accurately translated the word means more than just *"brother"* or *"brothers."* It literally means *"brotherhood."* This exemplifies what is called in Greek grammar, a *"collective singular."* Thus the emphasis of the term transcends the plurality of the *"brothers,"* to focus instead on the <u>oneness</u> of those *"brothers"* who are subjected to similar sufferings with our own. The thrust of this term, then, is that they have become a *"<u>band</u> of brothers."* They have been <u>bound</u> together by the common <u>bond</u> of suffering. Therefore, the word has the force of *"a fraternity,"* *"a community,"* *"a clan,"* or *"a guild."* A collective singular is a word describing *"a united whole."* [2]

The emphasis of such a term is on the shared conflict of all believers. No individual believer is in the struggle alone. Each one is at the same time defending, and being defended by all the others. Our conflict with Satan is tribal warfare. We must trust fellow tribesmen, and they should find us trustworthy as well. The nature of the struggle of all Christians is that we are in a fight with the evil one, but none of us are in this fight alone. If one member of the brotherhood fails to be faithful, all members are negatively affected.

The Third Great Principle of Victory

That leads us to the third great principle of victory – <u>mutual encouragement and accountability with other believers</u>. We need each other, and God expects us to be there for each other. God has determined we should play a vital role in each other's spiritual life and development. That is why Hebrews 10:25 warns us about *"not staying away from our meetings as some habitually do";* instead we should be *"encouraging each other, and all the more as [we] see the day drawing near."* God intentionally put us together for a purpose. As we face the inevitable trials, troubles, and tragedies of life, God intends that we should be supported, strengthened, encouraged, and empowered through the community of believers. As we face the challenges and temptations of life, we should receive support from one another. The Alpha Predator loves to catch us in an isolated situation. He loves to catch us alone.

God's purpose for us is a unified whole. We need each other. We need a fraternity of faith. The closer we stand in community, the more we will be able to bear up under the attacks of the Alpha Predator. Throughout our daily lives, and especially during tough times, God desires to strengthen and empower us through the brotherhood of believers. He expects us to support each other during and through the challenges each of us face. That is why we need to be an active part of a body of believers. We need others and they need us. Together we make up a tribe of faith. This is the key to the vital third principle of victory.

Hebrews 3:13 says, *"Encourage each other daily, while it is still called **today**, so none of you is hardened by sin's deception."* The nature of temptation is deception. Sin promises much but delivers little. The community of faith is a tremendous ally for each believer in overcoming the devil's ploy. Through fellow brothers and sisters, who make up the fraternity of the faithful, we are encouraged to live a life of righteousness and avoid the temptations of sin. Our mutual encouragement and accountability is "a difference maker" in each of our lives.

ALPHA PREDATOR

A Lesson Reinforced By a Long Walk with Brothers

Early one morning a knock came on the door of our house in Kamativi. When I answered, I found a group of BaTonga men waiting to see me about what they later described as *"an issue of considerable importance to us and our families."* After culturally obligatory greetings all around and a moment of pause in respectful silence, their spokesman began with their request. *"Mufundisi, we come from the village of Kenjobo. Do you know where it is?"*

Admittedly, I had heard of it. But, I had never been there. What I did know about Kenjobo is that it is one of the most remote villages anywhere in all of Tongaland. To this day, I have never entered a BaTonga village more logistically difficult or more topographically challenging to reach. Just to get there, a person has to traverse approximately eleven miles of thick African bush on a narrow path beginning from an outlying spot on the nearest rural road. And the journey from that starting point still involves crossing two mountains and a river. Then Kenjobo, itself, is located right on top of a flat-top mesa with rugged cliffs on every side. It gives new meaning to the concept of *"an out-of-the-way location."*

"Well, Mufundisi, we have heard that you have been sharing God's Word and have been showing a bioscope, The Jesus Film, in various villages throughout Tongaland. We want you to come and show the bioscope in our village and tell us the stories of God's Word as well. We have never had a white man to visit our village, and the people of our village have never seen a bioscope. Please come

and show <u>*The Jesus Film*</u> *in our village and give us your message from God."*

That one took me by surprise! I had not imagined they were going to invite me to come to their village to share the gospel. I began to fumble for my answer. And believe me, I can "fumble with the best of them" in English, but, you have never seen anyone really "fumble" until you see me "fumble" in ChiTonga when English is my first language. Finally I got my thoughts together. Too far – too remote – too logistically difficult to reach: all these things came rushing to my mind. At last, I spoke.

"First, I want to thank you for coming here. I am happy to hear you have a hunger for the Word of God and for <u>*The Jesus Film*</u>*. I would love to come to your village and I thank you for the invitation. However, in order to show the film, I would have to bring the projector, the generator, the viewing screen, and all the other equipment required for the presentation. There is* <u>*no road*</u> *to your village, and it would be impossible for me to reach your village with all that equipment without a road. If there were a road, it would be an entirely different matter. But since there is no road for the truck, I simply cannot come."* I smiled to myself and breathed a small breath of relief. *"Now, that should do it. That seems like a logical, yet rather loving and kind way of expressing it. It's just too far to go and too difficult to reach."*

Surprisingly, they said little at that point. They offered no argument even though obviously they were more than slightly disappointed. As an alternative, I invited them to come to other villages in the valley where I would be sharing the gospel and showing *The Jesus Film* in the upcoming weeks.

Over the next few weeks, a small number of the people from Kenjobo showed up at various places where I traveled throughout Tongaland sharing a gospel message and showing the film. Sometimes they trekked fifteen miles from Kenjobo just to be present! Impressive! Sometimes twenty, thirty, even fifty miles from Kenjobo! *"Wow! These people are really serious. They are really hungry for the Word and they really want to see the film."*

A month passed; then two. They were still sending the faithful Kenjobo delegation. Some of them had made public commitments of faith in Christ by now. Some were even staying away from their homes for days at a time in order to participate in the discipleship follow-up meetings I would hold in different villages for Biblical training opportunities for the people who had made professions of faith during our evangelism services.

Three months had now passed. Then one morning another knock came on my door. When I opened the door, there the Kenjobo delegation stood once again. By now I knew them by name. So after general greetings, I said to the group's leader, *"Daniel, I am pleased to see you men. How can I help you today?"* Daniel smiled, and lifting the crude Tonga Ax he held in his hand, he said, *"Mufundisi, the road is ready now. We have made a way for your truck to come through the bush to Kenjobo."*

The next day I made my way out to that remote spot where the nearest rural road led to the path leading through the bush to Kenjobo. I could hardly believe my eyes. There, through the bush was a cleared "road" – as far as my eyes could see! Daniel was there to meet me, and he said, *"Mufundisi, the road is cleared all the way to our village. Now will you come and preach the gospel and show the bioscope?"*

There was nothing else I could do. I said, *"I'll be there next Friday night!"*

The next Friday morning I turned off the rural road that goes to Binga and headed south on the "new" road to Kenjobo. Young men from the village were waiting for me there, and they sang songs of celebration as they walked in front of the truck as we made our way to their home. Occasionally, they would bend down to chop a small tree with their axes, leaving a stub in the road. Since these stubs were soft and green, the truck tires rolled over them without any problem. Sometimes the young men would stop and point out an elephant track. Once they even stopped to point out the track of a lion, and they mentioned there had been some lions spotted in the area recently. After several hours of travel on the "new" road, including digging our way out of a very sandy riverbed and crossing the two mountains, we arrived at last at Kenjobo.

Upon our arrival, there was more excitement among the children of that village than among any BaTonga children I had ever seen. At first I could not understand their unusual enthusiasm, but then it occurred to me. The reason for their excitement was they had never before seen a white man. The elation was shared by the entire village.

For the next three days we had a great time of ministry and of sharing the Word of God. Many of the people professed faith in Christ Jesus. I showed *The Jesus Film* twice, with more people in attendance the second night than the first. It seemed they just couldn't get enough.

Then, Sunday came. We spent the whole morning in a celebration service. We had much to celebrate. We could find no one left in the village who had not professed faith in Christ!

By 3:00 o'clock in the afternoon we had finished our lunch, had said our "goodbyes" and had begun to make our way back down the mountain, traveling on the new "road." In our company now, there were two young African men – Ndebele Machipisa and Beto Tshuma. They both lived near me in Kamativi and were now serving as my helpers. My son Rye was also along for the trip. He was thirteen years old at the time.

Even with the new "road," travel was slow and hazardous. After we had journeyed for about two hours, we had made only about a third of the distance back to the "main" road. As we rolled slowly along, the soft green stubs had now turned rigid, brittle, and sharp. Those sharp stubs made our travel like traversing a mine field. About 5:00 o'clock in the afternoon the first stub made its way through the tire. "*Psshh!*" No problem! We have two spares and there are three young men to help change the tire. After years of life as a bush missionary, one becomes experienced at these things. Twenty-five minutes or so and we would be on our way again. Everything was still going according to plan, until another five minutes had passed – then "*Psshh!*" Not to worry! The experienced Mufundisi had enough foresight to put in an extra spare! Another twenty minutes and we were on our way once again!

But, the delays were now beginning to take a toll on our schedule. It was just after 6:00 PM. It would be dark by 6:15, and we were still about seven miles from the road leading back to "civilization." (Not civilization, mind you – but at least the road leading to it!)

Thankfully, I had recently installed those new "super-duper" spot lights on the roll bar behind and over the cab of the truck. *"Lord, I am so thankful for your provision through those faithful women's mission groups back in America who are so thoughtful to send gifts like these!"* That night promised to be a great time to try them out. We would have to be very, very careful though. No more spares, and seven miles still to go – most of it in the dark!

Then we heard the most dreaded sound heard in the deep bush of Africa! Not the hissing of a cobra, or the overhead hacking chainsaw growl of a leopard, but the *"Psshh!"* of a deflating tire when we'd used all your spares, just as dark descended.

We drank the last of the water just before we left the truck to begin our long walk out. I recall wishing that we had just a little more!

I then looked at my son, Rye who by now was thinking about the Kudu Pizza we would be missing. Mother would have it waiting for us when we got home. *"Son, don't worry about it. It will be OK. Hey! It looks like it's going to be quite an adventure. We may be a little late getting home, but it's going to be all right."* Secretly, I too was thinking about Shirley's Kudu Pizza. It was going to be a long walk – an extremely long walk!

As best I could figure, it was about seven miles back to the main road from where we were at the time, and then another twenty-five miles back to our home in Kamativi. One thing was apparent to everyone now. We were going to be more than just "a little late." We were going to be really late. So I drew a deep breath and let it out slowly. The pulsing puffs of air set the pace for our long, dark night's trek.

We had walked about forty-five minutes when we heard the first elephants. It was dark now – not just suburban dark, but that *"you can barely see where you put your foot in front of you,"* kind of dark. We slowed our pace to make sure we weren't going to walk right into the middle of the herd. We carefully navigated our way around them, and after a considerable time of cautious skirting, we skillfully found the clearing of the "new road." (Code talk for – Thanks to the goodness and mercy of the Lord while we were rambling around in the bush as lost as wild geese in a snowstorm, we once again stumbled upon the cleared path that I had, under my breath, been desperately begging the Lord to help us to find.) *"Why did tonight, of all nights, have to be a night without a moon?"*

We continued our hike at a snail's pace down the side of the first mountain and then into the riverbed. We had traveled another hour by now, and I estimated we had about five miles yet to go before we would get back to the "main" road. There, in the riverbed, we took a break and sat in the cool sand. Since it was the dry season, no water was flowing, and the sand wasn't even damp.

As we sat there we joked about the great adventure the Lord had provided. Our talking relaxed and a tranquil mood came over the whole crowd. *"Guys there is just something about chilling out in the cool sand of a riverbed that helps get things into proper perspective. Things aren't so bad after all. We'll still make it back. It is all just a matter of ti . . . ."*

Then we heard the sound! My words were cut off in mid-sentence. Immediately we all got very quiet! *OUUURRAHH! OUUURRAHH! OUUURRAHH! RAHH! RAHH! RAHH! RAHH!* Forget what I said about the sound of a deflating tire being the most dreaded sound in the deep African bush. If you've ever heard it, you don't have to ask. LIONS! Real lions! Real wild African lions! And they were not so far away.

No one dared speak a word. I was now looking straight at Beto and Ndebele, but I could no longer see their teeth shining against their handsome black faces. And, it hadn't gotten darker, either. They just weren't smiling anymore. Their lips were sealed. The only sound among us was our adrenaline-induced heavy breathing, and that invisible stethoscope in our minds that always involuntarily kicks in when a person tries to suppress his heartbeat.

Ndebele was the first to break the silence. *"We must stay very close together, Mufundisi. The lions may not attack us if they see we are a group. Lions are more likely to attack when they see you are alone."* I nodded, and whispered, *"I think you are right, Ndebele. At least we will be safer if we stick closely together. David Livingstone, himself, would not have survived his attack by a lion had it not been for the presence of the faithful African people who were with him that day at Mabotsa."*

I should have expected the question. *"Who is David Livingstone, Mufundisi?"* Beto had been the one to voice it. Someone had to. We sometimes forget the context of differing historical backgrounds. So, after a quick lesson in evangelical missiological history, I concluded simply by saying, *"Even the great Livingstone needed others as he traveled. Though we read much about Livingstone doing this, and Livingstone doing that, in the end and in truth, it was Livingstone and company who accomplished what is written in the history books. He could have accomplished very little if it had not been for the faithful African people who were always at his side."* Ndebele then spoke, *"And now is it Musungwaazi and company?"* *"Yes, Ndebele. It has always been Musungwaazi and company!"* At that, both Ndebele and Beto smiled again. I said, *"Twiinde moonse." ("Let's go, everyone."*)

We decided to leave the "new road" path and cut directly across country. That turned out to be a mistake because our pace was slowed by the thicker bush and rougher terrain. Occasionally we would hear the lions roar as we walked along, but they seemed to be farther away each time we heard them. When we finally got back to the main road, I glanced at my watch. It was 12:20 AM, and we were staggering as much as walking by then. It had taken us almost seven and a half hours to make the trip. We still had twenty-five miles to go, but it had become evident by then I was walking with "a band of brothers." I was so grateful to God for this "fraternity of the faithful!"

We still had a long way to go and we still faced many challenges before we reached Kamativi the next morning. That night's grueling experiences reinforced a vital lesson in each of us. We need each other, and God expects us to be there for one another. It is the third principle of victory over the Alpha Predator – mutual encouragement and accountability with other believers. That is why Peter writes, *"knowing that the same sufferings are being experienced by your brothers in the world."* We are not alone in the fight, and neither should we try to fight alone. When we neglect the significance of community – the accountability, responsibility, encouragement, and fellowship of brothers and sisters in Christ, we set ourselves up for failure and defeat. When it comes to an attack from the Alpha Predator, we need others. This battle is tribal in nature and we should never try to engage in it alone. We need to stick together!

SUMMARY: Part One How to Be Victorious

In the introduction to this book I related the story of the death of David Pleydell-Bouverie. His was a tragic death resulting from an African lion attack in the deep bush of the Matusadona wilderness area in Northwestern Zimbabwe. In that introduction I made the statement, "the young man died for all the wrong reasons." That statement is, in fact, the absolute truth. As we look back over the three principles of victory when we are attacked by the Alpha Predator, as presented in the first section of this book, it is easy to see David Pleydell-Bouverie violated every one of those principles and the resulting cost was his life.

Principle number one: *"Be sober! Be alert!"* – You better be constantly watching. David Pleydell-Bouverie left his tent fly open even though he was warned by his safari guides not to do so. He was careless. He was not alert. He was not watching. There is victory in vigilance, and his lack of it cost him everything.

Principle number two: *"Resist him, firm in the faith."* – Fight back with everything you've got and refuse to run! Witnesses to the last few moments of Pleydell-Bouverie's life, said they saw him running from his tent after the attack began. When he ran, he was ruined.

Principle number three: *". . . knowing that the same sufferings are being experienced by your brothers in the world."* – Mutual encouragement and accountability with other believers is essential to a spiritually victorious life.

We need each other, and God expects us to be there for each other. We need to stick together. The nature of our battle is tribal. God does not mean for us to fight alone. Perhaps Pleydell-Bouverie's biggest mistake was pitching his tent a considerable distance from the other campers. When he separated himself from the remainder of the group, he set himself up as easy prey. He had spent the day with the others. Many of them were his friends. But he weakened his defense considerably when he neglected the safety of his tribe. The violation of each of these principles opened the door wider and wider for the fatal attack.

Spiritually speaking we can learn much from the tragic experience of this young man and from the principles of defense outlined in Peter's warning. When the Alpha Predator attacks, we need to be certain our lives line up with these great truths. *"The Devil is prowling around like a roaring lion looking for anyone he can devour."*

The spiritual lives and testimonies of countless believers have been devastated, and in some cases practically destroyed, simply because they have failed to heed this warning of Scripture. The Lord has been gracious to share these principles of victory with us and to give us these tactics of defense when it comes to an attack from the evil one. However, if we ignore these strategies of protection, we do so at our own considerable detriment. Ask anyone who has been mauled, mangled, or battered. He will tell you quickly, the price paid is never worth the neglect!

PART TWO: Life's Ultimate Adversary

TAYLOR

CHAPTER 4 Facing The Facts

"Your adversary the Devil" (1 Peter 5:8b)

The most prolific man-eating lions of all time roamed and terrorized a 1,500 square mile area of southern Tanzania, known as the Njombe district. Between the years of 1932 and 1947, this pride of fifteen claimed hundreds of lives. At least 1,500 people were killed and devoured, and perhaps as many as 2,000. George Rushby, the British game warden who was responsible for hunting them down and who at last brought an end to their reign of terror, wrote, *"The renowned man-eaters of Tsavo were very small fry compared to what these proved to be."*

In June of 1956 George Rushby retired as the Deputy Game Warden of Tanganyika. Upon his retirement, he and T.V. Bulpin, the author of his biography, commenced preparations for the writing of a book that would tell his life story. In 1962, the book was first published in Cape Town, South Africa, under the title of The Hunter Is Death. It tells the story of how Rushby hunted down and destroyed the most diabolically productive man-eaters in the history of the world. A copy of the book sets on the bookshelf behind my desk, along with other books on Africana and adventures of that faraway land.

Many episodes of sheer terror are described in the book. Perhaps none are more descriptive and exemplary of the dreadful horror inspired by these lions than the events that occurred one night in the village of Mambego when the Njombe pride strolled in and began to wreak havoc among the people living there.

At the time of the attack, George Rushby had been hunting the man-eaters approximately fifty miles away from Mambego. When he heard of the carnage that had transpired in that village, he immediately moved to Mambego to hunt there. Arriving at the village, he found it was in a state of total chaos. Most of the inhabitants had run away. In the confusion of the ravaging assault the only people remaining were the old, too feeble to escape, and the extremely young who had been left behind by their fleeing families. In addition, numerous scattered lifeless corpses gave evidence of the efficiency of the lions as horrendous killing machines bent on wiping out all signs of life and resistance.

Being respectful of African ways, as George walked into the village, he shouted, "*Hodi*," which is the indigenous way of knocking on a door. It literally means, "*May I come in?*" The only person in the entire place able to respond was a little girl. She answered in the local language, "*Come near*." In the commotion of that dreadful night, it seems she had been overlooked by her parents when all her family had escaped.

She would discover later they all had not actually escaped. Her mother had been caught and eaten by the pride just a few yards from their home. Now, as Rushby and the little girl sat in the shade of a tree, she began to recount the events of the previous night.

She described how when the lions had attacked the village she had been sleeping under a blanket in the center of a hut. As the lions pounced on the roof, some animal skins left drying by her mother above her head had fallen on top of the blanket, further hiding her and masking her scent. Petrified with fear at the sound of all the screaming going on around her, she had actually lain silent and motionless under her unlikely disguise until the sun had come up and the lions were finally gone.

As I read the account, I began to imagine the sheer horror the little child must have experienced as she waited through the long hours of darkness of the African night. She could hear the low snarling of the carnivores as they crept around her on every side. She could clearly perceive the moist and soggy chewing sounds of the brutes feeding on the freshly slain bodies of her friends and family members. She listened in disbelief as she realized those with whom she had been sitting around the evening fire just a few hours before were now being devoured only inches from where she lay cowering and alone.

She cringed as one of the creatures came near and pawed softly at the leather hides covering her face, curiously sniffing and testing them for aromatic integrity. The animal paused as it took time to speculate why these pelts from the African plains were contaminated with such a strong and pungent scent of humanity. She was certain the brute must be able to hear the beating of her heart. To her, it seemed to be pounding with the volume of the night drums. Why couldn't she silence the sound of her labored breathing? Despite her attempted suppression of it, in her mind it was now roaring like a windstorm in the butterfly-shaped leaves of the mopane trees. As she held her breath, the sudden fear of suffocation sieged her thoughts. She curved her lips around her teeth in an effort to stifle a full breath. But her abbreviated attempts at exhaling and inhaling only prevented the gratification of her desperate need for air. Each short breath fell just shy of satisfaction.

Would she be next? Would they discover her soon? Would those sharp yellow-white daggers in the mouths of these butchers of the bush snap her neck as quickly as they had those of the others? Or, would she die slowly?

This was torture – true mental anguish and torment. Heartbeat after heartbeat, minute after minute, hour after hour – time was dragging like coagulating molasses caught in a slow motion video. It was agonizing. Her terror had become more than she could bear. Nevertheless, she had to bear it if she wanted to live. So she wept – but she wept in silence – frozen in fear like a shackled dreamer wrapped in a cerebral straitjacket, unable to move in the plot of her dream, paralyzed in the restrictive clutches of a nightmare.

Many times during the horrific hours of that ghastly night she wanted to scream and give vent to the tension of the terror trapped in her mind. She wanted to throw back the concealment under which she was hiding and just run away until she could run no more. But facing the facts of the situation in which she found herself, she remained still and silent under her coverings, realizing such behavior was her only chance for survival.[1]

While her behavior is remarkable conduct for an eight-year-old girl, let me be quick to add, it is entirely consistent with the actions I observed in the lives of the children of the rural Africans among whom I lived in the deep bush of the Zambezi River Valley. It seems they have an uncanny ability for exhibiting mature behavior far beyond their years. Perhaps that is the result of the parental training they receive from their earliest years. Their parents teach them early in life to acknowledge that they live in an extremely unsafe part of the world. Lions, snakes, and elephants, as well as many other potentially dangerous animals are a real part of their environment and the possibility always exists for an up close encounter. These are the facts of life in the African bush. Parents train their children on how to give a proper response should such encounters occur.

As children of the Most High God, we could learn much from these bush children and their extraordinarily mature approach to life. We too, at least spiritually speaking, live in an unsafe environment. If we are going to be victorious over our adversary the Devil, we, too, must face certain facts.

Fact Number One: Life is a Battle

If we are going to please God with our lives, it is important for us to view life from God's perspective. And if we are going to understand life from God's perspective, we must begin to see it as the Bible reveals it. When we read God's Word – in both the Old and New Testaments –

71

we quickly discover the Bible defines life for the believer as a continuous struggle. We are in the midst of a battle for our souls. Life is a conflict, a combat, a continuous invisible warfare. According to the teaching of Scripture, the primary arena for that battle is within the individual. Our battle is a spiritual battle, and the conflict relates primarily to matters of the heart. In Ephesians chapter 6, Paul makes it clear that we do not *"battle against flesh and blood, but against . . . spiritual forces of evil."* The clear teaching of Scripture is that these *"spiritual forces of evil"* are headed by one called *HaSatan* – Satan. He is the devil, the ruler of this world, the Prince of Darkness – the Alpha Predator, life's ultimate adversary.

While there are delights of victory along the way, life by and large is a perpetual conflict, and if we are going to view it properly, we must begin to see it as it really is. Life for the believer is a combination of the challenge of combat and the thrill of triumph. In fact, as we examine Scripture, we discover the life that is revealed therein is much like fighting lions and eating honey.

Fighting Lions and Eating Honey

There was no sound as the lion crept furtively through the scrub toward the young man who was making his way down the path. His flattened body and tawny coat produced a perfect palette of camouflage as his frame fused with the colors of the grass. Nothing about him divulged his presence to the man. His only contrasting features - the jet black markings on the back of his ears - were invisible, facing as he was toward the man. As a cub those spots had served to help his mother locate him in the tall grass. Now they only served as defining décor, like a feather in the headdress of a warrior.

The lion's target was a tall and handsome man, with bulging arms and a chest like a wedge firmly resting on the circumference of his waist. He was muscular and tan with the look of worldly sophistication: the perfect picture of an outdoorsman who obviously enjoyed competition and games. His hair was long and flowing, not unlike the Italian fashion model Fabio. And he was a ladies' man, too. But the lion had no interest in the young man's physique or appearance. His interest was in the textured protein of his flesh, and the beast licked his lips as he imagined an easy meal. He had even noticed there was no weapon in his quarry's hands. Imagining his meal, the lion had to suppress an instinctive growl as he sized up his prey.

As the man approached closer, the lion's ears spontaneously dropped against the back of his skull. He gathered his hind feet under his haunches, claws grasping the earth like the racing spikes of a runner preparing for a sprint. He was now ready for his charge. Two more steps and the man would not stand a chance. Just two more steps and the prize would be his.

That's one! That's two! Now!

The lion's supple body exploded from the bush like a muted muzzle-flash from a high-powered rifle. The young man never saw him coming. But the roar at his right was almost deafening as the lion sprang through the air and connected with his meat-hook appendages digging deep into the young man's torso.

For a moment there was a jolt of fear. But then something came over the young man, and he caught the lion with his right hand between the fangs of the lion's upper jaw and with his left hand between the fangs of his lower jaw. With a surge of phenomenal strength, he tore the lion's jaws apart like *King Kong* ripping apart the jaws of the Tyrannosaurus Rex in Academy Award winning director Peter Jackson's 2005 film by the same name. This unexpected victory resulted from a unique response to a lion attack to say the least!

I'm sure you have determined by now what I have just described is not a "typical" African lion attack story. In fact, the story does not come from a lion attack in Africa at all. It comes from the Bible story of Samson as found in the Old Testament book of Judges. The Bible tells us the phenomenal strength that came over Samson was the result of the Spirit of God Who came over him and equipped him with strength unlike that of an ordinary man. Otherwise, it is highly unlikely he would have stood a chance defending himself against a lion with his bare hands.

Samson, of course, is a name that has become synonymous with extraordinary strength. His birth was miraculous and his strength came as result of the Spirit of God on his life. He was one of three men in Scripture who operated under a life-time Nazirite vow – a unique vow of separation and consecration to God. In his case, the vow was symbolized by long, flowing, uncut hair. He was a man of tremendous capacity and extraordinary strength, but his potential was marred by his uncontrolled appetite for women and worldly pleasure. Repeated failure was the pattern of his life because of this unchecked spirit.

In spite of his many failures, however, numerous events in his life have much to teach us about the nature of the Christian life. In fact, I have often said if you want a snapshot of the life of a believer and the perpetual occupation of his daily experience, you should just turn to an incident in Samson's life as found in the book of Judges, chapter 14. There we read the Biblical record of the story I shared above. We pick up the narrative a few days after Samson's victory over the lion.

He was on his way back home now after visiting a girl in the Philistine town of Timnah. This was not just any girl, I might add, but the famous Delilah, of the Philistine make-shift barber shop fame. When he came to the place where the battle had taken place, he spotted the remains of the lion. We are told the lion's carcass had become dry, and inside the carcass a swarm of bees had built a hive full of honey. Samson reached into it and scooped out big handfuls of the sticky sweet stuff.

Now, if you are following the story, push the "pause" button on the mental video presently going through your mind. Look at the still picture of the man standing before you. He is a young man, perhaps with parallel crop-row scars running the length of his bulging muscular arms – wounds left there from the sharp claws of a lion. But as he stands there, look closely at what is dripping from his hands. It is honey! And, a celebrative smile is on his face as he eats some of the wonderful tasting delicacy.

I am convinced that picture is a concise illustration of the Christian life. Day after day we find ourselves both fighting lions and eating honey. While the believer's life is a conflict, a combat, an on-going battle; there is also daily rejoicing over the victory that is ours in Christ Jesus and celebration of the fruit Christ brings into our life along the way. A life of fighting lions and eating honey is a beautiful picture of the nature of the Christian experience!

Catching Fish and Bailing Water

It was a picturesque Zambezi morning with no wind on the lake. Obviously, a little BaTonga boy had inherited his father's discarded dugout canoe. He was not old enough to have a dugout of his own, and the condition of the boat gave away the fact someone must have abandoned it.

Shirley and I had slept the night before on the boat provided by the International Mission Board for reaching the remote River Tonga people. It was a twenty-one-foot cabin cruiser and we draped mosquito nets from the canopy covering the open floor at the back where we placed blow-up mattresses for a bed. We had awakened with the sun and we were watching the little fellow as he paddled slowly down the lake and pulled his small boat into the peaceful inlet where we had been sleeping. We sat quietly on the back of the boat, less than twenty-five yards from where the little guy was fishing. He was attempting to secure some small Kariba bream to provide a breakfast feast for his family.

The only sound was the occasional "bloop" of the fishing hook, weight, and line on the end of his crude pole being cast into the tranquil water near the edge of the lagoon. Sporadically he would pull in a fish, take it off his line, and then re-bait his hook. But he would also bend down with a small metal dish and bail water out of the boat. That is when I determined that his dugout must have been an "inherited" one. It was apparently leaking like a sieve. So, there we sat watching him – catching fish and bailing water. I turned to Shirley and said, *"You know, that is a perfect picture of the Christian life – catching fish and bailing water!"*

Every day during our mission years we experienced the delight of participating in the harvest of the Lord. We were catching fish, and we rejoiced in this ingathering into the Kingdom of God. But also every day we were bailing water. Sometimes this water "bailing" came in the form of just staying afloat by meeting the challenges of daily life in a place like the Zambezi River Valley. Sometimes this water bailing came in response to a direct assault from life's ultimate adversary. Occasionally he planted snags in the course of our journey. Sometimes he scored a direct torpedo hit by slamming some major trial into the hull of our lives. But always, it seems, while we were catching fish, we were also bailing water.

That is the pattern of life for every faithful believer. The first fact we must face is that life is a battle. Sometimes fighting lions, sometimes eating honey, sometimes catching fish, sometimes bailing water, but always life is a battle.

Fact Number Two: We Have an Adversary

If this, then, is the real perspective of the Christian life as revealed in Scripture, it should come as no surprise to us that Satan, as the great Alpha Predator of our souls, attacks us and distracts us in every way he possibly can. In the early part of verse 8 of 1 Peter 5, Peter uses two words to introduce us to the nature of our spiritual nemesis. He refers to him as the *"adversary"* and the *"Devil."* These two words highlight our understanding of the spiritual enemy of our souls.

The word translated *"adversary"* in the original language of the New Testament is the word *"antidikos,"* and it is actually made up of two words in the Greek language – *"anti"* meaning *"against"* and *"dike"* meaning *"a lawsuit."* While it is a word originally used to describe an opponent in a court of law, over its years of usage it began to lose its strict legal meaning, and it became a word used to describe any enemy or adversary. Strictly speaking, it describes anyone who is actively and continuously hostile toward another person.

Focus on the first part of that word *"antidikos."* It is *"anti,"* and as seen above it means *"against."* Do you ever get the feeling that everything is going *"against"* you? That feeling may not be the result of spiritual perception. It may rather be because of pessimism or even because of a negative attitude bordering on paranoia. The truth is, not everything in this world is set against you, so get real. However, while that is the case, it is also true, if you are a Christ follower, there is someone in this world who is always set against you. He is Satan, the devil, the ultimate adversary, and if you are a believer, he is <u>always</u> against you in everything you do. He is against your joy. He is against your peace. He is against your testimony. And he is against your witness. He is against everything that is good and pure and righteous and holy and healthy in your life. He is the ultimate adversary of your soul and he is "*anti*" to every good and wholesome thing about you.[2] Commentator Marvin R.Vincent writes, "*It is the very essence of the devilish nature to oppose Christ.*"[3] If you are Christ's follower, you can expect the opposition of this adversary, as well. He is against you. Face the facts. He is "*anti*" to everything Christ-like in your life.

Fact Number Three: Our Adversary is an Accuser

The other term Peter uses to describe this Alpha Predator is the word "*Devil.*" In the original language of Scripture, the word is "*diabolos.*" That is a more familiar word, and it actually means "*accuser.*" It, like "*antidikos,*" is a compound word, and it is formed from two Greek words – "*dia*" meaning "*through*" and "*ballo,*" meaning "*to throw.*" This word pictures what the devil does. He "*throws accusations through*" a person's life. He "*riddles him with allegations.*"

The "*diabolos*" is one who picks holes in a person's life and who spreads criticisms and innuendos. He does this not only by bringing false charges against an individual but also by disseminating the truth about the person in malicious, insidious, and hostile ways.[4]

Sometimes what he has to say about us is absolutely true. When he says that I am weak, it is because I really am weak. When he says I fail, it is because sometimes I really do fail. But he deliberately says it in such a way as to hurt and damage. The accusations of the evil one may not always be "false" accusations, but they are always malicious and intended to hurt or destroy.

That is why we can rejoice that we have "*an Advocate*" One who pleads our case before the Father – One Who can say, *"While it is true that this child is a sinner, this child has failed, this child is the epitome of weakness; it is also true that this child is a blood-bought, blood-washed, blood-redeemed child who belongs to Me – I have taken away his sin and imputed unto him My righteousness. Therefore, Satan has no case."*

Revelation 12:10 describes the end time and the ultimate defeat of Satan, but it also tells us about the daily occupation of Satan, *"the accuser of our brothers has been thrown out; the <u>one who accuses them before God night and day.</u>"* This passage describes the devil's continual activity. Every day, night and day, the Alpha Predator attacks us by accusing us before God.

This continual accusing is exactly what happened in Job's case. Satan said to God, *"The only reason Job serves you is because you pay him to. Remove your blessings and he'll curse you to your face."* In our life, like in the life of Job, Satan continually tries to point out our "bad side" to God – to make us look bad in God's eyes. He wants to manipulate our lives with guilt and to destroy our effectiveness and our peace with God.

"Remember the Duck"

Once, a little boy was visiting his grandparents on their farm. They gave him a slingshot to play with, but told him to use it only in the woods. He practiced in the woods, but he could never hit the target. Getting a little discouraged, he headed back to the house for dinner.

As he was walking back to the farmhouse, he saw his grandma's pet duck. Just out of impulse, he let it fly, and hit the duck square in the head and killed it. He was shocked and grieved. In a panic, he hid the dead duck in a woodpile only to look up and see his sister watching. Sally had seen it all, but said nothing.

After lunch that day Grandma said, "*Sally, let's wash the dishes.*" But Sally said, "*Grandma, Johnny told me he wanted to help in the kitchen today, didn't you, Johnny?*" And then she whispered to him, "*Remember the duck?*" So Johnny did the dishes.

Later, Grandpa asked if the children wanted to go fishing, and Grandma said, "*I'm sorry, but I need Sally to help make supper.*" But Sally smiled and said, "*Well, that's all right because Johnny told me he wanted to help.*" And she whispered again, "*Remember the duck?*" So Sally went fishing and Johnny stayed home.

After several days of Johnny doing both his chores and Sally's, he finally couldn't stand it any longer. He came to Grandma and confessed that he killed the duck. She knelt down, gave him a hug, and said, "Sweetheart, I know that. I was watching out the window and saw the whole thing. Because I love you, I forgive you. But I was wondering just how long you would let Sally make a slave of you."[5]

Paul writes in 2 Corinthians 5:19, "In Christ, God was reconciling the world to Himself, not counting their trespasses against them . . ." The good news of the gospel, for all of us who trust in the finished work of Jesus, is that God does not count our sins against us. He counts our sins against Christ!

Perhaps that is why Peter writes with such authority on this subject. He was in a unique position to know and understand this truth. After all, we all know what he did.

He failed the Lord miserably. On the night before His crucifixion he denied Him there by the enemies' campfire, and you can rest assured Satan never let him forget it. No doubt he continually accused Peter before God. But he also accused Peter to Peter. With a thousand agonizing reminders Satan brought the matter to Peter's mind again and again.

The result – Peter was devastated. He couldn't get back up. He couldn't get that terrible thought out of his mind. He couldn't imagine it would ever be possible for him to serve the Lord as he had previously been able to serve. But Jesus had other plans for Peter. After forgiveness and restoration He wanted him to go on with his life once again.

Remember the Rooster

In fact, He had tried to prepare Peter for this devastating experience when He shared with him at the Passover. In Luke 22, He had said to him, "Simon, Simon, look out! Satan has asked to sift you like wheat. But I have prayed for you that your faith may not fail. And when you have turned back, strengthen your brothers . . . . I tell you Peter . . . the rooster will not crow today until you deny three times that you know Me" (vv. 31-34).

We all know what happened next. Even though Peter rejected the idea that he could ever deny the Lord, he did deny Him. And the rooster did crow. And the crowing of that rooster reminded Peter of the Lord's words, and the effect of that remembrance was shattering. For Peter it was a reminder of the certainty of his sin. Christ had declared it would happen just as it did.

But what Peter overlooked was that the crowing of the rooster was also an invitation to repent. It seems he had forgotten the other thing that Jesus had said. The Lord had also said, *"When you have turned back, strengthen your brothers."* Christ saw the inevitable denial coming. Yet He saw beyond the denial to repentance and restoration.

Satan wanted Peter to wallow in his guilt, so he bombarded him with perpetual self-accusation. Christ wanted Peter to dare to believe again, so he saw beyond the guilt to restoration and renewal.

Here is a question: As it relates to man, what is the primary purpose of the crowing of a rooster? The primary purpose is not to convict of sin. The primary purpose of the crowing of a rooster is to announce the dawning of a new day!

That's exactly what Christ wanted Peter to learn. No failure is final. No sin so severe that one cannot start again with Christ. Satan will accuse you continually, but Christ wants you to deal with it and go on. Satan's purpose is to knock you out of the race permanently, but the Lord wants to strengthen you through your experience in order that you, with a greater appreciation of grace, may be able to go on, and in turn strengthen others, as well. Satan wants to rip you to shreds, but Christ wants you to continue to grow as the person He desires you to be.

How grateful we can be that Romans 8 begins with these words: *"There is therefore now no condemnation for those who are in Christ Jesus . . . ."* and ends with these words, *"For I am persuaded that neither death nor life, no angels nor rulers, nor things present, nor things to come, nor powers, nor height, nor depth, nor any other created thing will have power to separate us from the love of God that is in Christ Jesus our Lord!"* (vv. 1, 38-39)

Look at how that passage begins and how it ends. It begins with *"no condemnation,"* and it ends with *"no separation."* For those of us who are *"in Christ,"* there is *"no condemnation"* and there is *"no separation"* – we are kept safe forever – regardless of what Satan has to say. It matters not whether his accusations are false or true. God assures us that He alone has the final word!

Each one of us should be so thankful for that great truth. Life can be so painful, and the experiences of life can be so ruthless. I've experienced some of this ruthlessness myself. I'm sure many of you would have to say that as well.

I know what it is to fail. I know what it is to fall on my face so badly as to wonder whether I could ever get up again. I know what it is to be the brunt of Satan's lies – to be falsely accused –to be tempted just to give up on the race forever. But I also know that the *"God of all grace"* is sufficient to overcome whatever "the accuser" may have to say. That is our heritage as children of the Most High God.

You're Not Out, Until God Says You're Out

Our enemies may laugh at us. Our friends may become disillusioned with us. Those who are closest to us may give up on us. The evil one, himself, may assume we are thoroughly defeated. But it is God, the Father, Who has the last word. And we are never finished until He says we are finished.

One of the well-known professional baseball umpires of the 1930's and 1940's was a guy by the name of Bill Kleim. He was a colorful personality – and considered by many to be at that time, the loudest mouth on the east side of the Mississippi River.

Once he was working a game at Yankee Stadium between the New York Yankees and the Cleveland Indians. The score was tied 2-2 and it was the bottom of the ninth inning. The Yankees had a man on at second base when Gil McDougall hit a single to center field. The Cleveland outfield quickly retrieved the ball and fired it back to the catcher. The catcher applied the tag just as the runner slid across home plate. It was a close call. All over Yankee Stadium for a few moments it became completely quiet. But then from the Cleveland bench and from the stands, the team and their fans began to shout *"He's out!"* But the Yankee bench and all their fans shouted – *"No! He's safe!"*

The whole stadium seemed to be involved with conflicting screams *"He's out!" "No, he's safe!" "No – out!" "No – safe!"*

Finally Bill Kleim stood up and held his hands up high. *"Quieeeeet!"* He shouted at the top of his voice. Then he took off his mask and said, *"He ain't nothing until I say what he is!"*[6]

That accurately illustrates the authority of God when it comes to our sin, our failure, and our restoration. Right now, Satan may be trying to knock you out of the race. You may be ready to give up and quit. You may be so discouraged that you think you will never be able to effectively serve the Lord again. But remember, *"You ain't nothing until God says what you are."* And you're not *"out"* until He says you are *"out!"*

Our opponent, the "devil," is our enemy. He is life's ultimate "adversary." He is the Alpha Predator – the great lion intent on the destruction of our soul. He is real and he is ruthless. And he'll bad-mouth you every chance he gets. But it is the Our Great God Himself Who has the last growl. And the final victory is ours through Christ Jesus, our Lord.

So, forget about the "singing fat lady!" Face the ultimate fact. The final word belongs to the Father of Lights! You're what He says you are. Don't ever forget that!

CHAPTER 5 A Terrorist On Tiptoes

"prowling around like a roaring lion." (1 Peter 5:8c)

OK, it's "quiz" time. Is the lion the loudest animal in the bush or the quietest animal in the bush? How many say the loudest? How many say the quietest? How many say both? Those of you who guessed "both," are probably the closest to being correct. A lion is an acoustical contradiction – he is an anomaly of volume – being both very loud and very quiet, often at very nearly the same time.

On a still night, the sound of a lion roaring in the bush can be heard from more than five miles away, and if he is only 50 yards away, the volume is so loud it can make the metal panels on a truck vibrate in response.

Probably the sound most people associate with lions is the growl of the MGM lion at the beginning of movies. But you need to understand, that is not a full-blown roar at all. That is more like a sneer than a roar. An all-out roar is a deep and dangerous sound. In fact, the roar of a full-grown African lion at close quarters is the most awesome sound I've ever heard in nature, and believe me, with all the sleeping outdoors I've done in the deep African bush, I've been in a position to hear lots of sounds.

I recall sleeping one night in a little bush residence in Africa where a lion was roaring not more than twenty feet from the back wall of the house. I could actually feel the lion's roar as it made the house tremble. On another occasion, I was sleeping in a tent in a secluded bush campsite where a lion was roaring nearby. Every time the lion would roar, I could look above my face and see the tent fabric quiver as it reverberated with the sound.

Previously I mentioned that in my library I have a collection of many turn-of-the-century African hunting books. Among those books is one written by Sir Alfred Pease written during the first decade of the Twentieth Century. Though written in the first couple of years of the 1900's, it was not published until 1913. There were two tragic reasons for the delay. First there was a delay because of the death of Pease's wife after thirty years of marriage. But the delay was also because of the death of his dear friend, George Grey, who was killed by an African lion right before his eyes.

The volume is entitled *The Book of the Lion*, and it is considered a true classic in the annals of "Africana." It is renowned among literary historians for its accuracy on lions and lion hunting, and particularly so, for a book published so early. In that book he describes, rather colorfully, the roar of a lion.

There is no sound which issues from the throat of any creature to compare with that of the lion's voice. Heard near at hand in the dark or in daylight, his roar is a truly terrible and earth shaking sound. It gives awful notice to every living creature that their king is walking the silent night to deal out death. And while it strikes with terror on the ear of every creature of the forest and wilderness, it cannot fail to impress the listening man with awe and often with dread.

Why do lions roar? Why do they announce their oncoming in the night, or their departure, as with bloody lips they leave their horrid work in the cold dawn? Do they roar after their prey? Do they roar from pangs of ravening hunger? Are they challenging or calling or courting or just defying all creation? Or is it the outcome of mere boastfulness, making all this noise? I do not know.

I hear them on dark nights when they are turning the plains into shambles as they prowl among the whitened skulls left from a hundred cruel previous feasts. But I hear them too in the morning, when the first sunlight is slipping quietly forward over the hills, and the vultures are gathering for their turn. But still, more often I hear them about an hour or so before dawn, when they have had their fill of flesh.[1]

The Rule of His Roar

The roar of a lion is actually a sound-based demarcation of the lion's territory. In fact, resident males only roar when they are in their own territory. It is a display of ownership and declaration of possession. This territorial claim of a roaring lion is both in the geographical sense, an area of land, and in a chronological sense, a specific time of day.

What do I mean by "a chronological declaration of possession?" I mean lions rule the night! They are predominantly nocturnal predators. Most hunting by African lions takes place at least under the poor light conditions of early evening or dawn, but especially during the night. What is the reason why they prefer the darkness? Eyesight! The size of a lion's eyes is much bigger than that of humans, and lions need only one-sixth of the light humans need to be able to see. Their preference for darkness is also in keeping with the true Jekyll and Hyde character of their nature. During daylight hours they will usually move off fairly quickly if disturbed by humans or even a medium sized dog. However, once the sun has gone down, there is not much on this planet that a lion fears. In the dark they undergo a radical personality change.[2]

Is that not an accurate picture of Satan, the Alpha Predator? *Just* like an African lion, Satan, the Prince of Darkness, prefers night over day. In fact, Satan's domain and territory *is* the kingdom of *darkness*. His rule in his kingdom domain consists of principalities, powers and rulers of darkness. But, when we are saved, we respond to truth and receive clarity. We are transferred from darkness into light. The Bible describes this transformation in the following way: *"He has rescued us from the domain of darkness and transferred us into the kingdom of the Son He loves, in Whom we have redemption, the forgiveness of sins"* (Colossians 1:13-14). We are rescued from the rule of Satan's roar and are established in Christ's realm of radiance.

ALPHA PREDATOR

A Connoisseur of Concealment

But amazingly, a lion can also be the quietest animal in the bush. The lion is what is known as a "digitigrade" animal. Essentially that means they walk on their toes. This makes them so quiet that when they walk they make no noise at all.[3] They are literally "terrorists on tiptoes." They are masters of stealth and easily sneak up on their prey.

I was once within ten meters of a lion in the long grass of a remote bush area, and I never even knew he was there until he jumped up and revealed himself. Add to surprise the fact his coat is the same color as the sun-dried grass of the African plains. These characteristics make it possible for him to slide across the savannah without any detection whatsoever. And remember the fact he usually hunts at night and the darkness is actually his preferred hunting environment. His final charge toward his prey is often made from no more than ten yards, and it seldom exceeds twenty. All these traits play to his advantage and combine to make him the master of covert attacks. Many times his prey does not even know he is nearby until it is too late.

When he begins his stalk, every fragment of cover separating him and his quarry is used. He will often freeze and remain totally motionless if necessary in order to escape detection. Prey is normally attacked from behind and the killing bite is usually directed to the back of the neck. No wonder Peter compares Satan to this great apex predator of the bush and the plains. The Alpha Predator's intimidation and deception are prominent features of his perpetual stalk and assault of humankind.

Deception

The devil is sneaky and he prowls about looking for victims to trap with his devices. Deception is his ceaseless activity. He is constantly on the prowl. He is always looking for opportunities to undermine our Christian walk. He uses deceit and cunning to accomplish his task and he is just as dangerous in the spiritual realm as a lion hiding in the long grass is dangerous in the physical realm. Deception is one of his primary tools. The goal of the Alpha Predator is to deceive you by beguiling your senses, perverting your judgment, enchanting your imagination, and giving you false views of spiritual things. He wants you to think you are "having a good time" by enjoying sin for a season, but in reality he is deceptively destroying you in the midst of that enjoyment.

Years ago while living in Zimbabwe I heard how some rural Africans find water when none seems to be available, either because of draught or some other cause of scarcity. Though I have heard many different versions of the story, I was told an African man will sometimes take a small shiny object and hold it up high in the air where it catches the glint of the sunshine off its surface. He will do this in the presence of a baboon who is watching him from his perch in a tree. Then the man will take a sharp stick and drill a hole in the side of an anthill, reaching the hollow center of the anthill. He then takes the shiny object and pushes it into the hole until it drops down into the bottom of the hollow anthill. All of this is being observed by the baboon, who is one of the most curious animals of the bush.

After the man has done this, he walks away and conceals himself, watching to see what the baboon will do. The baboon begins to think about the shiny object and about possessing it as his own. Assuming the man has left the area, the baboon walks over to the anthill and reaches his hand deep inside and down until he grasps the object. His only problem is now his fist, with the object firmly secured in it, is too large to withdraw. So, he begins to tug desperately at his hand in an attempt to free it. He screams and he pulls, but he overlooks the one thing he most needs to do. He will not let go of the object, and so remains trapped by it.

Meanwhile, the man approaches the baboon with a noose and places it over the baboon's neck. Now, in fear and panic, the baboon lets go. But it is too late. The baboon is trapped. He has been duped.

Then the man leads the baboon with the makeshift leash to a tree and secures him to it with the leash. Periodically he tosses him a chunk of salt, and the baboon assumes he is still winning because all the salt he can eat throughout the afternoon doesn't seem like such a bad deal. By late afternoon the salt is beginning to take its toll and the baboon is terribly thirsty. At this point the man sets the baboon free. Again, the baboon thinks he is still winning, but because he is so thirsty, the first thought on his mind is to find something to drink. He takes off running as fast as he can for water.

The man doesn't know where the water is, but he knows the baboon knows where the water is since the simian survives in the bush every day. The man follows the baboon and finds him drinking at the water. At that point, the man disposes of the baboon and takes the baboon's water for himself. That trickery is how he secures water when he has no other way to find it.[4]

The inevitable question – why doesn't the baboon just let go? Why don't we? Deception is one of Satan's most effective tools. That is the way of the great Alpha Predator. He lies in the grass and waits; then with deception he pounces when we least expect it. And he often starts off by offering us something "shiny."

It can happen to any of us! Even the strongest of us, spiritually speaking, can be deceived if we are not on guard. That is why Peter begins his passage with *"Be sober! Be on the alert!"* We must always be watching!

You see, it is commonly believed that lions attack mainly the sick, the wounded, or the old. But that is simply not the case. Animals in their prime are also often taken by lions. Lions are opportunist hunters, and after a careful stalk, they will take the closest animal regardless of it age, sex, or condition. They do not test their potential prey for weaknesses like other predators, such as wild dogs, do. They will take any animal in range regardless of its condition. Whichever one can be deceived becomes a potential target. Deception is a primary means of effectiveness and success.[5]

Years ago, clever Native Americans, hunting in Alaska, understood this principle and in like manner employed it when stalking wild game. For example, when an Eskimo wanted to capture a wolf, he would first get a sharp knife and coat the blade with several layers of dried or congealed blood. Then he would take that knife and bury it in the snow with the blade sticking up out of the snow. The wolf, roaming the area, would eventually smell the blood and come to the knife. Soon, after sniffing its attractive aroma, he would start licking it. At first he enjoyed the taste of the fresh blood clotted on the blade of the knife, even though it was cold and coagulated. But, as he licked more frantically the blood began to taste even fresher, and he noticed it was no longer cold. He was delighted to find himself licking fresh warm blood. He thought he had discovered the source of a feast, but from the wounds of his now shredded tongue he was essentially consuming his own life. He soon died from blood loss on that very spot. He actually bled to death, the victim of deception.[6]

That is exactly the way Satan attacks many people today? He offers something appealing, and at first those thus deluded think they have uncovered a feast. But later they realize they are victims of an execution by deceit.

The Alpha Predator is a master of treachery. He is a terrorist on tiptoes and he will do anything necessary to stalk his way into your life. He is *"prowling around like a roaring lion looking for someone he can devour."*

Intimidation

The word translated *"roaring,"* in the Greek language is the word *"oruomai,"* and it is a word we often refer to in the English language as an onomatopoeia. An onomatopoeia is a word derived from the sound the word is describing – like the *"hisssss"* of a snake, or the *"meow"* of a cat. *"Oruomai"* sounds somewhat like the roaring of a lion. And it is a word that especially denotes the roar of an animal with fierce hunger.

As we have seen, sometimes a lion will sneak up on its prey and capture it with deception. In fact, deception is one of the lion's primary tactics. But sometimes instead of deceiving its prey, a lion, will frighten its prey and thus immobilize its victim with consternation and confusion. At this point, a lion's roar becomes his weapon. What the devil cannot accomplish through allurement, he often tries to achieve through foreboding and fright.

Truly, fear is one of the major impediments to living an uncompromising Christian life. Just like a lion intimidates by his roar, the devil intimidates many through fear. Fear incapacitates the believer and prevents him from moving ahead in his Christian walk. That is why the Alpha Predator loves to roar!

Let me pause to ask a significant question. What do you think is the number one most common command found in Scripture? It might surprise you, but it is not to be more loving. That may be the core of God's desire for human behavior, but it is not His most frequent decree. Neither, does His most frequent directive have anything to do with conquering vanity or acquiring humility, and, surprisingly, it is not even about guarding sexual purity or walking with integrity.

The single command occurring in Scripture more often than any other is simply this – *"FEAR NOT!"* *"Do not be afraid. You can trust Me. Be strong and courageous. Fear not!"* In fact, there are 366 *"fear not"* verses to be found in the Word of God.

Why do you think God stresses that statute so much? Why do you think He commands us not to fear? Why does He tell us to stop being afraid more than anything else He has to say? The reason is simply this: God says *"fear not"* so often because fear will sink you faster than anything else. Fear disrupts faith, and it becomes the biggest obstacle to trusting and obeying God. God says *"fear not"* so often because fear is the number one reason human beings are persuaded to disobey God. That may well be why Satan roars so often. He wants to intimidate us out of doing what God want us to do.[7]

You cannot walk by faith and live in fear at the same time. In fact, you cannot walk with God for any length of time without facing your fears.

The Cautious Never Live At All

I don't play golf or tennis, and I don't collect stamps. So, when I want to relax and do something for fun, I really enjoy spending time with horses. Fortunately, over the years, when we weren't living in Africa, my family and I have lived either in New Mexico, Oklahoma, or Texas. All of those places are great places to live if you enjoy American Quarter Horses. And in most of the places where we have lived, there have been generous individuals who have made it possible for me to own and keep at least one young colt or filly of my own. This has been a joy, and nothing is more relaxing for me than working with and training a young horse on a cool fall afternoon.

One Wednesday night, shortly after we returned from Africa in 2001, our youngest daughter McKelvey and I were driving to church, and we were enjoying our time together. Whenever McKelvey and I talk casually, sooner or later it seems, our conversation comes around to a discussion of horses.

Perhaps this goes back to our days in Africa. We had no television there, probably the best thing that ever happened for our family life! We learned to read and play games together. And I told our children made-up stories. One of the characters of one of those oft repeated stories I invented for McKelvey was a beautiful mahogany bay horse I called "the Chocolate Rocket." Long rambling stories of the superb coffee-colored colt helped pass the time as we made our four-hour journey through the bush to the nearest grocery store from our house in Kamativi, Zimbabwe.

The great thing about fictional horses is that they sometimes have no faults. This thought must have been in McKelvey's mind as we spoke that night on our way to AWANAS. She paused in our conversation and then spoke with a tone of seriousness. *"You know, Dad, I would really like to ride Saga."* She was referring to a new dark bay, Doc O'lena/Peppy San Badger colt I had recently purchased, which was fully charged with the speed and athletic ability of the legacy of his ancestors. He was like the mythical "Chocolate Rocket" except he was real and he was dangerous, so I quickly tried to discourage her desire. *"Now, honey, Saga is not just an average horse. He is fully loaded and could be very risky for you to ride. I don't think it would be a good idea for you to ride him just yet."*

She turned her face toward the window and just sighed. Then she spoke softly as she looked right at me again. *"You know, Dad, the brave may not live forever, but the cautious never live at all!"* I found out later she was actually quoting a line from *The Princess Diaries*, but at least, she got my attention with her remark. *"The brave may not live forever, but the cautious never live at all."* Fear can destroy your spiritual life.[8]

Have you ever noticed every time an angel shows up in Scripture he always seems to begin the conversation by addressing the same subject? Invariably, it seems he begins the conversation with the words *"Fear not!"*

There is only one apostolic prayer recorded in the book of Acts. But, have you ever noticed how that single prayer concludes? It ends with these words, *"Lord, consider their threats and give your servants courage to speak Your name with boldness."* (Acts 4:29)

Why do you think the apostles prayed for boldness? There's only one reason – they were afraid! The enemies of Christ, who had been so relentless in their pursuit of Him, were now on their trail, too. So, they asked God for help.

But notice what they were asking for. They did not ask God to eliminate their enemies or even change their state of affairs. They asked Him to give them resolution to do what they knew they had to do.

God wants us to be bold. And that is why the Alpha Predator tries to frighten us so much with his roaring. He wants to frighten us out of the effective work of God.

Do you hear his roar? It may not sound to you now like you imagined it would sound. Sometimes it sounds like this: *"You've blown it too badly this time."* *"You'll never overcome the disgrace of this experience."* *"You'll never conquer your past."* *"You're too weak to ever do a work for God, again."* *"You might as well just give up."* *"You'll never be restored."* *"Your situation is hopeless."* You're *doomed*!" That's how the roar of the Alpha Predator sounds. He wants you to be afraid. He wants you to be very afraid. He wants you to be so afraid that you just quit, bolt, and run away.

But if you listen to Satan's roar, and if you give in to a mindset of fear you'll find yourself at the end of your life one day, sitting somewhere in an innocuous and benign place of compromised retreat and withdrawal asking yourself questions like *"What might have been? If I had just trusted God, what might I have done? If I had not given in to fear, what might I have become?"*

Every one of us will sooner or later face those moments when we must choose between trust and fear. God will always call you to something bigger than yourself. But you will never know God is trustworthy if you don't risk obeying Him even when you are afraid. *"Trembling yet trusting"* is the final definition of true courage.[9]

Facing Down the Intimidator

At the time of my writing, the average life expectancy for a man living in Zimbabwe is 37 years of age.[10] Orders Chasungwa made it just a couple of years beyond that mark before he died. One day, shortly before that time, Orders and I made our way far up the Zambezi River. After traveling for several hours we turned northwest and headed up a smaller river called the Lufuwa. It was a fascinating trip traveling up a deep rocky canyon for the next couple of hours, the echo of the boat engine sounding like the soundtrack from the *African Queen*. At the base of the gorge, on each side of the river there were indigenous villages scattered all along the way. The structures therein were remarkably natural with no sign of the impact of outside influences.

As the river began to narrow I pulled the big cabin cruiser into a shallow place where it would be hidden from sight by the trees and vegetation lining the bank of the waterway. We unhooked the small "dinghy" I always pulled behind the bigger boat and began to make our way further up the river. The dinghy was a small shallow boat approximately ten feet long, and I had a four horsepower motor fastened on the back. After loading the camping gear and food, the total water clearance on the sides of that little boat was only about six inches.

By the time we had traveled another six miles or so, the evening shadows were beginning to darken the gorge, and the barking of the baboons began to ricochet off the canyon walls like vocal gun shots. At the sound of the boat, excited little rag-clad children ran down to the edge of the river. Some shouted, *"Mukuwa, mukuwa!"* – *"white man,"* *"white man."* I realized some of them had never seen a white man before.

By the time we neared the mouth of the final and still smaller river of our journey, it was completely dark. Orders was shining a big spotlight I had hooked to an old car battery setting in the bottom of the boat. The eyes of curious animals were now visible all along the river bank as they reflected in the light. Those of the bush babies looked like sparks coming off a fire as they ran through the trees.

But then there, stretched all the way across the mouth of the Lusungazi River was a giant Nile crocodile. Menacing and intimidating, he was easily a time and a half as long as the dingy, so I estimated 15 or 16 feet in length. His eyes, reflecting the beam of the torch, looked like the taillights of a '56 Ford – big, round, bright red eyes. His dagger-like teeth overlapped on the top and bottom of his narrow-snouted broad jaws in a cynical buck-toothed smile – the characteristic larger fourth tooth of his lower jaw always visible even when his mouth was closed. Oddly, the ridges on his powerful tail protruding high above the water reminded me of the roofline on the Sydney, Australian Opera House.

He was big. He was formidable. And, like a fixed and obstinate barricade, his body blocked admittance to the river we had to enter in order to get to the village where the Lord had led us to preach the gospel that night. I switched off the little motor, and for a moment gathered my thoughts as I listened to the sweat ooze out of the pores across my brow. Should I try to wait him out? What if he refuses to move?

After collecting my thoughts, I realized there was only one thing to do. It's not what I wanted to do, but it was the only thing I could do. I pulled on the rope and started the engine. I then engaged the gear, and headed straight for the crocodile. At first he was motionless and refused to move. But when the boat got so close to the massive reptile that I feared it might touch him, the big crocodile rolled away. Flexing his tail, he hurled water up and over the boat, dousing both Orders and the apprehensive *Mufundisi* sitting in the back of the dinghy, who was now conspicuously a "whiter shade of pale."

Orders, screamed in ChiTonga, *"Tili kukufwa!" "We're going to die!"* For a moment I wished I couldn't understand the language – I had found Orders to be about ninety percent right in most situations. Presently, however, it was too late for turning back. There was nothing to do but face down the intimidator. Full speed ahead!

Of course, by now you've figured out that unless this book is being written by a literal "ghost writer," we made our way safely to the village that night and I preached the gospel. Scores of people were saved. Today there is a church located in that remote place far up the Lusungazi River. The alarm of the moment didn't last long. Once I started the engine, it was all over in about ten seconds. But the lives that were changed that night are going to live forever. What if we had decided not to go? What if we had decided to turn back because of the crocodile? What if we had listened to Satan's roar and let him intimidate us out of a work for God?

You'll never know that God is trustworthy if you don't risk obeying Him even when you are afraid. *"The brave may not live forever, but cowards never live at all!"* *"Fear not!"*

TAYLOR

CHAPTER 6 That Intentional Look In His Eyes

"looking for anyone he can devour." (1 Peter 5:8d)

Herbert Kashula was a giant. Not an actual, genuine giant like Goliath or even Andre', but, nevertheless, a big man. When I first met Herbert Kashula, he owned and operated the Antelope Park just south of Gweru, Zimbabwe. These days, I'm told the park has grown into quite a tourist attraction, complete with luxury chalets, elephant rides, and nature walks with young lions. But, originally, the park was rather basic. Back then the Antelope Park experience was essentially a quiet afternoon of driving on winding roads during which time a person could see various African plains game, *manenge* baboons, and various other fauna of the African bushvelt.

In those days the star attraction was a big male African lion affectionately known by Herbert and other locals as "Joe." He was a beautiful specimen – muscular and sleek, with a dark black mane and tail tip, and huge ochre eyes. His enclosure was surrounded by an eight-foot-high fence –

minimum security for such a capable prisoner. When I looked at the size of the lion compared to the height of the fence, I always imagined how easily he could have escaped if he had really put his mind to it. But, for some reason, he never did. He seemed to have settled that issue somewhere and somehow long before.

Each afternoon Herbert would feed Joe, and the big cat's meal usually consisted of the hindquarter or front shoulder of an antelope, zebra, of if necessary, a domestic cow. Lions eat meat – and plenty of it. There are no such things as giant economy size cans of Alpo for the king of beasts.

I loved to be there at feeding time. Though I could not often make it because of my own schedule, when I could be there, I always enjoyed watching Joe respond to the meat. After all, placing fresh, red, raw protein near an African lion is like flipping an electrical switch after connecting the terminals to the head of Frankenstein's monster. The listless ogre suddenly comes to life. Regardless how unengaged, inactive, and unanimated he may have been before; suddenly his actions rapidly and abruptly change when the meat comes. His eyes now begin to glare. His pace now becomes intense. His frame now is fluid. *"He's alive! He's alive! The creature has come to life!"*

Every afternoon the scene was repeated. Day after day and week after week, Herbert Kashula would approach the enclosure and lift a huge chunk of meat high above his head, holding it there at the top of the fence. Joe would then leap up, and much like an athletic NBA superstar slam dunking the ball in the last period of a lopsided game, he would hang his paw over the fence and linger as if in frame-freeze mode when his massive claws sunk deeply into the meat. Quite a spectacular sight!

This happened so often and with such regularity, Herbert Kashula got very use to the routine. In fact, he had become so comfortable with his role as the "setter" and Joe's role as the "dunker," occasionally his hand would actually reach the level of the top of the fence. But one day something occurred that changed his relationship with Joe forever.

That day, Herbert Kashula lifted the meat, and at the same time Joe leaped into the air and his huge paw came over the top of the fence as it always had done previously. But this time the result was entirely different. Instead of sinking his razor sharp, meat hook shaped claws into the texture of the venison; one of those claws sliced straight through the back of Herbert Kashula's hand and came out the front like an inelegant and reversed version of a man whose hand had been pierced in a crucifixion.

From that point, the situation worsened rapidly. Kashula quickly released the meat, but the weight of the man and the weight of the lion on opposite sides of the fence suspended each of them on their tiptoes, resulting in both of them being clumsily slammed together in a face to face encounter with only the mesh of the wire fence separating the two. At that proximity, the stench of the lion's breath was overpowering and the volume of the lion's roar was deafening. Though extremely painful, it was a merciful and welcomed relief when seconds later the lion's claw ripped through the webbing beneath the skin between Kashula's fingers and he fell to the ground.

Later recounting the experience, Herbert Kashula said to me, *"I tell you, Steve, I don't believe Joe ever intended to hook me that way, but once it had happened, I can assure you from looking straight into his eyes with nothing separating us but the wire of that fence, he didn't just want to scratch me up a bit, he wanted to destroy me completely. I could see that intentional look in his eyes!"*

When we read the words of Peter in his warning in 1 Peter 5:8-11, it is easy for us to spot *"that intentional look"* in Satan's eyes, too. In fact, in verse 8, Peter tells us that Satan is *"looking for anyone he can devour."* That is the intentional and determined purpose of the Alpha Predator.

Frank Herbert, the author of the *Dune* book series, has one of his characters say at one point in the story, *"I must not fear. Fear is the mind-killer. Fear is the little-death that brings <u>total obliteration</u>."*[1] The goal of Satan for the believer's life is the <u>total obliteration</u> of his effectiveness. The Bible says he wants to *"devour"* us – he wants to *"swallow us down."* That is his ultimate aim and ambition. That is the intentional look we see in his eyes.

Perpetual Surveillance

The word translated *"looking for"* is the Greek word, *"zeteo."* It means *"to go in search for,"* *"to strive to find"* or *"to try and discover."* The verb form used here points to continuous action. Our adversary's *"search and destroy"* mission is constant.[2] He is always looking for an opportunity to trick us, to trip us up, or to overwhelm us. The devil will continually do all he can to retaliate against God by defiling our lives and ruining our testimony. He is always looking for any opportunity of advantage that he may employ to hinder our effectiveness.

He is crafty, he is cunning, and he is always looking for someone to destroy. He is on a constant search and destroy mission. That is the vital strategy of his plan. It is his primary occupation. He does this day and night. It is the intentional look in his eyes.

In the Old Testament, Satan looked for and found Job and then petitioned God regarding Job. On the day when he presented himself before God, God asked Satan where he had been. His answer is significant. *"From roaming through the earth and walking around on it."* (Job 1:7). Satan is continually roaming around on the earth looking for someone he may destroy, and when he finds someone who is vulnerable, he moves in for the kill.

In the New Testament, Satan looked around and found Peter. He even asked God for permission to *"sift Peter like wheat"* (Luke 22:31). This is what Satan does. He is looking twenty-four hours a day, seven days a week, 365 days a year for people who call themselves committed followers of Christ, and he wants to *"sift them like wheat."*

Isn't it interesting that when Jesus came, He stated His purpose as having come to seek sinners? But, when Satan comes, he comes looking for saints. He is looking for Christians living with a mindset of complacency. When he finds them like that, he does everything within his devious power to reduce them to ineffectiveness. His mission is a constant search and destroy mission.

Maswera Sei

One night, Orders Chasungwa and I were camped in an exceptionally remote location of the Simatelele area of the Binga District in the Zambezi River Valley. After a successful evangelism service held earlier that evening, the people of a nearby village were beating drums in order to keep the hippos from entering their fields and raiding their crops. The beating of the drums also had a secondary, yet welcomed effect in that it prevented the hippos from coming near, and from interrupting the pleasant dialogue the *Mukuwa* missionary was having at the fire with his helper.

It was an enjoyable evening with a gentle breeze blowing softly from the lake. Waves melodically lapped against the shoreline, and in the distance women chatted softly around their own gender-specific fire, occasionally disrupting their pleasantries to chase down a child who wandered beyond the ring of the firelight. They were taking advantage of a rare moment of relaxation and respite from their never-ending busy schedules, while the men of the village hounded the hippos. The combination of these simple sounds produced a soothing symphony – the effect of which had the same calming ambiance as elevator music, albeit in a much more pleasurable and enjoyable environment.

The scene was set for a prolonged and gratifying conversation, and Orders and I talked long into the night. As the hours passed and the fire burned low, the exchange became more and more somber.

For a while we spoke about the hippos. They seemed to be everywhere that night. We discussed how the hippo is responsible for more human fatalities in Africa than any other large animal. The male hippos aggressively defend their territories, which run along the banks of rivers and lakes, and the females have also been known to attack violently anyone they sense coming in between them and their babies, who stay in the water while their mothers feed on the shore. Hippos are built for destruction, and they can run at speeds of over twenty miles an hour and have enormous jaws which host canines up to twenty inches in length. A large hippo can grow to be up to thirteen feet in length and stand five and a half feet tall at their back, weighing more than 7,500 pounds. They are remarkable creatures and capable killing machines the size of a SUV.[3]

But somehow that night, as we spoke of animal attacks and ultimately of death, the subject changed from hippos to lions. As we spoke, Orders leaned in closer toward the fire. He took a piece of *mwenge* wood and placed it on the glowing embers. (The BaTonga people all know the qualities of this wood. When it is added to a campfire, it will cause the fire to glow with the intense illumination of an incandescent light bulb.) After adding the *mwenge* wood, he shook his head and clicked his lips as he often did whenever he was thinking of something terribly dreadful.

"*Musungwaazi,*" [*tsk,tsk,tsk,tsk,*] "*it was awful. There was one lion they called Maswera Sei. He tried to kill all the people. He was a mean one, that one! And he killed many people near our village at Negande.*"

Orders Chansungwa had grown up on the eastern side of Tongaland near the village of Siakobvu, in Chief

Negande's area. It is an area that even today is still as wild and remote as any place on earth. Many nights while traveling on the primitive bush road in that area, I've been delayed while I've waited for huge herds of elephants and Cape buffalo to cross. It can be a spooky place when you're all alone at night and when you realize there is not another human being for miles in either direction all along that lonely bush road. It is a land of thick mopane forests and deep Kalahari sand. It is a land of piercing night sounds punctuated with long deep impaling periods of silence that can cause a man to tilt his head, questioning his auditory senses; pondering whether the thick stillness is the product of loneliness or simply the vast expanse. And this was the land of *Maswera Sei*, the man-eating lion of Chief Negande's region.

I found myself thinking, *"Maswera Sei?' What an unusual name for a lion,"* That term – *Maswera Sei* – is not a personal moniker normally used for a name, at all – neither human nor animal. Instead it is the term the Shona people use for their usual afternoon greeting. That being the case, I asked Orders to explain why they called the lion *Maswera Sei*.

Again he shifted the crude carved wooden Tonga stool on which he was sitting and once again leaned in closer to the fire. Now he was looking around like a teenager telling ghost stories at summer camp. The flashes of light from the smoldering *mwenge* wood danced across his face and reflected the yellow-orange hue in the edges of the whites of his wide bright eyes.

"Mufundisi, [tsk, tsk, tsk tsk,] it was because of how that lion always showed up. Every afternoon just as the

shadows got long and dark at the base of the big mopane trees, he would find someone walking alone. Suddenly, without any warning whatsoever, he would spring on that person and the person would be gone."

"One day, a young girl walking home from our school said 'so long' to her friends, and was left alone. They continued walking along the main road together, but she had to make her way alone on a path through the bush and across a river to her village several miles away. It seemed especially dark and quiet inside the deep bush that day. Huge teak, mopane, mahogany, baobab, and m'chibi trees hid the sun."

"The spoor from her footsteps, found later by the trackers, told the story. She must have been terrified. She was walking slowly, slowly, (mbuli camuntomwe) – like a chameleon," he said as his arms and hands went through a mimicking charade of a chameleon's pace. "Maybe she could hear him growling, or perhaps it was his footfall cracking the dry September leaves. But, they say from the evidence of her tracks, she never ran. He sprang off a rock near the path and his teeth pierced her throat and broke her neck. They said she probably never even had time to scream!"

"Musungwaazi, [tsk, tsk, tsk, tsk,] it always happened the same way! It was always in the afternoon. It was always when a person was alone. He was always looking for an isolated person like that. That was Maswera Sei!"

Maswera Sei was an <u>afternoon</u> opportunist. He was always looking for a person alone, but he always did his searching at a certain time of day.

In that sense, Satan is different. He does not limit his "looking" to a certain daily time frame. On the contrary, the word Peter uses in his warning tells us that the Alpha Predator's "*looking*" is continuous. It is perpetual. He is always "*looking for anyone he can devour.*"

Intentional Annihilation

The word translated "*devour*" in the original language is "*katapino.*" It is like many other words in this passage and is actually a compound verb made up of two other words. The word, "*kata*" is a preposition and it means "*down.*" "*Pino*" is a verb and it means "*to drink.*" So, when Peter puts those two words together to form one, it means "*to drink down*" or "*to swallow and swallow down completely.*" Figuratively, it means the "*complete and sudden destruction of someone or something – thus utter devastation.*"[4]

Peter's point is that the Alpha Predator is not merely interested in pawing his victims or scratching them up a bit. He doesn't want to just bloody their nose. He wants to completely devour them, to completely destroy their faith, so they wholly cease from walking in a vigorous way with God.

So don't be deceived, he is not interested in merely nibbling at you, he wants to gulp you down, and he will not be content until he sees you utterly devoured. Don't delude yourself into thinking Satan just wants to make you despondent. He will be pleased if you are discouraged and dismal, but that is not his ultimate goal. He wants to swallow you down completely. He wants to ruin your testimony, make you an ineffective Christian, and distort you for life. Annihilation is the aim of this Alpha Predator

The word *"katapino"* is used 36 times in the Septuagint – the Greek translation of the Hebrew Old Testament. The way the word is used clarifies for us what Satan wants to do to our spiritual life. A couple of Old Testament examples should suffice to demonstrate his intent.

For example, one of the early uses of the word in Exodus depicts the confrontation of Pharaoh's magicians with Moses and Aaron. We read, *". . . each one threw down his staff and they turned into serpents. But Aaron's staff swallowed up (katapino) their staffs"* Ex. 7:12). On another occasion we read that Jonah, the prophet of God was literally *"gulped down"* by a giant fish. *"The Lord appointed a great fish to swallow (katapino) Jonah, and Jonah was in the stomach of the fish three days and three nights."*[5]

From these uses of the word it becomes apparent that the intent of an animal or a snake when it swallows its victim is an accurate picture of what the adversary wants to do with the lives of the saints. He is bent on absolute and complete obliteration.

In some ancient Greek writings the word was even used to describe *"engulfing waves,"* like those of a tsunami. The picture that comes to my mind is a scene from *Deep Impact*, a science fiction disaster movie about meteors on a collision course with planet earth. A young female reporter makes her way to the beach to meet her father from whom she has been estranged. After a brief conversation with her dad, the Beitterman meteor, the first and the smaller of the two meteors scheduled to crash into earth, finally arrives. In the film it passes directly over the heads of the ill-fated couple. Then when it strikes the surface of the sea, there is a huge explosion resulting in the force of the detonation of an atomic bomb. As result, a giant tsunami rises up and begins to make its way toward the shore.

There they stand – this father and daughter in a loving embrace as the giant liquid swell towers hundreds of feet above their heads. As the daughter hides her face in his chest, the father takes a deep breath, facing the killer wave moving toward them now at a precipitous speed like a fluid avalanche. In a powerfully destructive instant, the reporter and her father are completely engulfed and wiped out in a moment. That's what it means to be *"swallowed up."* That's what it means to be *"devoured."*[6]

I'm also reminded of Psalm 124, where David writes about Jehovah's deliverance of Israel from the danger of extinction. As we read that passage, it becomes apparent how similar David's description of the danger threatening Israel is to that of Peter's description of Satan's intended destruction of Christians in his 1 Peter 5 passage. We read, *"If the Lord had not been on our side when men attacked us, then they would have swallowed us (katapino) alive in their burning anger against us. Then the waters would have engulfed us; the torrents would have swept over us. The raging waters would have swept over us. Praise the Lord who has not let us be ripped apart by their teeth."* (Psalm 124: 2-6) *"Katapino – to swallow down."* That was Satan's intention for Israel then, and it is his intention for us today. But it is a plan that was and is prevented through God's intervention.[7]

ALPHA PREDATOR

A Dramatic Predatory Reversal

I am so thankful this verb "*katapino*" is not only used in reference to the Alpha Predator. Sometimes in Scripture it is also used to describe the actions of our Heavenly Father. In fact, Paul uses this same word to explain "*when this perishable will have put on the imperishable, and this mortal will have put on immortality, then will come about the saying that is written, 'Death is swallowed up (katapino) in victory*" (1 Cor. 15:54).

Again, in one of the greatest prophetic promises found in all of Scripture, Isaiah records concerning God, one day in the great future, "*He will swallow up (katapino) death for all time, and the Lord will wipe tears away from all faces, and He will remove the reproach of His people from all the earth; for the Lord has spoken*" (Isaiah 25:8).

Satan may give it his best shot. His goal is to utterly destroy us. The intent of his gaze reveals his desire to swallow us down completely. But, the last gulp always belongs to God, and in the end, it is His plan to "*swallow up*" and reverse the destructive plot of our ultimate adversary.

Enter the Predator of the Alpha Predator

What do you eat for breakfast? Given the choice, I usually eat Rice Krispies or Lucky Charms, and I drink my first Dr. Pepper to start the day.

What do you think God eats for breakfast? I think He eats ANCIENT SERPENTS and DRAGONS, and He drinks down ALPHA PREDATORS instead of orange juice

117

just to make His day! (Revelation 20:1-3). I fact, I believe I can illustrate that fact with a real life story.

Satan Takes His Best Shot

The day began like any other in the lakeside village of Siavonga. Our family had not been to town for six weeks and that night we would be in Lusaka. There was tremendous excitement in the Taylor family's missionary household. Our plan was to buy our grocery supplies, purchase a few other things we needed for the house, then go out to eat at a real restaurant in the city. We had even already agreed on the place where we would be going – *Marco Polo's* – one of the finest dining out places in all of Lusaka, Zambia.

We arrived at the restaurant just before 7:00 PM, and I tipped the night guard generously so he would give extra attention to our truck with our groceries and supplies stacked in the back. We made our way inside and were ushered to a seat at a finely appointed table where we enjoyed a wonderful meal. For the next hour and a half, surrounded by the fineries of the remnants of an alien culture, Shirley, our youngest daughter McKelvey, and I escaped through an imaginary "rabbit hole" back into a world we had left behind years before – a land and lifestyle we had known prior to making our home in the deep bush of Africa.

Roused from our dream world by the reality of our need for rest, we left the restaurant just before 9:00 PM, and made our way back to the Missionary Guest House, located in a nearby part of town. We never suspected that we were being watched, or that we had become the targets of the intentional gaze of the evil one. But that night, the Alpha Predator had made it his plan to *"swallow us down,"* and he had inspired wicked men to be a part of fulfilling that intent.

We were driving our new heavy duty 4X4 recently provided for our family by the International Mission Board when I pulled into the drive and up to the gate of the Missionary Guest House. I thought it a bit strange that the inside night guard did not immediately respond to the sound of the blowing of the truck's horn. That was his signal to open the gate and provide entrance into the relatively secure grounds of the mission compound. Yet for some never discovered reason, the guard did not respond to the signal, and those few moments of delay set the stage for the dangerous events which unbeknownst to us were rapidly developing behind us at the time. I recall looking through the rearview mirror of the truck, seeing another set of vehicle headlights appear, and momentarily thinking to myself that other missionaries must be arriving at the same time.

Then I saw a very troubling image. Five men, each carrying an AK – 47 automatic rifle, became clear silhouettes in front of the headlights of the vehicle that now had us securely pinned against the gate. There was no way out! I only had time to grasp the gear stick between the seats and make an attempt to shift it into reverse. By that time, the first of the thieves was at the window of the truck with his rifle aimed squarely at my face. He motioned with the barrel of the gun for me to lower the window.

When I lowered it, he began to scream. *"Get out of the truck, white man!"* His muffled demand came from beneath a wool ski mask draped over his face and head. I spoke only once and said, *"Let my wife and little girl get out of the way and I will give you whatever you want."* I was determined not to budge until they were safely out of the truck.

"I'm going to kill you, you [expletive] white man!" I focused on the cavernous black hole in the end of the rifle muzzle, now only inches from my eyes. It was so close I could see the raised rifling lands inside the barrel, and I imagined the next thing I would see would be the red – orange flare of the muzzle flash. But then looking beyond the barrel my eyes locked momentarily with those of the thief, and for a moment I saw it – that intentional look in his eyes. He really intended to kill me. His eyes narrowed and he took a quick breath. I watched as his trigger finger tightened slightly against the trigger.

But then I heard him curse and hiss beneath his mask. For some reason he did not carry through. It was as if his plan had been prevented. Instead he motioned to one of his accomplices indicating that he should let Shirley and McKelvey out of the vehicle, and though the accomplice still held a rifle on them, I saw they were safely seated on the ground.

The door swung open and the man holding the rifle reached in to jerk me out of the seat. Again I didn't budge, but it was neither strength, nor courage, nor determination that held me this time. Both the thief and I had forgotten I was wearing a seat belt. With my neck now burning from the pressure of the nylon belt, I reached down and unfastened it. The thief and another of his accomplices immediately had me on the ground. They forced my face into the gravel as one frisked my pockets for money and valuables. The other held the muzzle of the gun against the base of my skull until it ached from the force. Then in a moment they were gone, taking with them the truck as well as our groceries and supplies.

That Feeling of Defeat

This was not the first time we had been robbed in Africa, but it was the first time involving such violence. Over the course of the next week, Shirley and I spoke often of it. There is something about the violation of theft that makes the experience difficult to get over. Those of you who have experienced it can readily identify with the feelings of desecration and defilement we felt following the event.

As we spoke over the course of the following days, we recalled the many ways in which we could see the Hand of God present in the midst of this dreadful incident. He was completely faithful to the promises of His Word, and He was in complete control of what seemed to be a series of out of control events.

It's Time to Do Something

By the end of the week I had related the episode at least what seemed to be a thousand times, and I was just about "talked out." Both fellow missionaries and African nationals asked us repeatedly to give the details, and I was weary of talking about the occurrence. I really wanted to do something about it. I decided the best thing to do was to go out and share the gospel.

I believe as a matter of principle one of the key components to restoration and recovery in a believer's life whenever he is facing depression, discouragement, and defeat, is to go out and share the gospel. A proactive sharing of the Word of God with others on the part of the Apostle Peter appears to be a prominent feature in the Lord's plan for his restoration. Three times in John 21, Jesus says, "*Feed My sheep. Feed My lambs. Feed My sheep.*" I am convinced when a believer is down, feeling defeated or victimized by the evil one, the best thing for him to do is to take the fight to Satan by going out and sharing the gospel with others.

This is what I determined to do in response to the satanic attack in Lusaka. All that was left for me to do was to determine the place where I would go. After much prayer I realized it had to be strategic and it had to be an extraordinary location with people in desperate need of the gospel.

How God Devours the Devourer

The name of the village had a wild and foreboding sound. They called the place *Sitali*. *Sitali* is one of the ChiTonga words for "*crocodile*." And I discovered later that the location lived up to its name. The area was full of crocodiles. It was also home to a community of people who had never in their history had the gospel preached in their village. I had been putting off going there simply because of the tremendous difficulty of reaching that place. It was so far and so inaccessible, but in light of the events of the week before, I had a burning desire to take the fight to Satan right in the midst of one of his most strategic strongholds.

The people at Nanjili had told me about the place several weeks before. Until now I had thought Nanjili was located at the end of the world, but Sitali was at least a half day further up Lake Kariba by motorized boat, and more than three days further by dugout canoe. Sitali was really "out there." And Sitali was the site I prayerfully chose for the rebuttal of Satan's presumed victory in Lusaka.

When I rounded the final curve in the big cabin cruiser, the scene was like what I imagined it must have been for Livingstone when he first explored this area more than 150 years before. Not much had changed about this village during the past century and a half. The inlet was completely hidden from view to anyone traveling on the main body of the lake. It was not the kind of place a person might just stumble upon. In fact, without the local guides from Nanjili I would have never found it at all. It was situated in an idyllic location, high up on a hill – the best place to catch a breeze, the best place to escape the mosquitos, and the best place to avoid the crocodiles.

The children began to sing and dance when they first saw the boat. Any touch from the outside for them was a rarity. This place was far from everywhere. No place I had ever been was near it, either in location or in time.

As the hull of the boat slid gently into the embrace of the sand, the beach at the base of the hill somehow transformed from a shoreline to a time machine. I leaped off the bow of the 21^{rst} century, but my feet landed firmly in the antiquity of the New Testament. The Book of Acts suddenly no longer seemed as distant as the pages of Scripture; it seemed as near as the questioning eyes of these time-bound people.

I made my way up the hill from its base to the summit. About half-way up the hill I noticed an enormous pile of stones just to the side of the path. When I inquired as to their meaning, I was told every time the people made their way up the hill, each individual would place a stone on the pile as a sign of respect to the demons in order to satisfy the spirits who dwelt along the path.

Walking into the village at the top of the hill, I noticed tiny shelters resembling huts near the larger actual huts where the people were living. When I asked about these, I was told they were lodgings for the spirits who inhabited the hilltop prior to the arrival of the people now living there. Animism, superstition, and fear were more prevalent in this place than any place I have ever traveled in Africa. As I looked around at the apprehensive yet inquisitive stares of the growing crowd I was reminded of the words of the writer of Hebrews as he described Christ as the One Who came to *"destroy the one holding the power of death – that is, the Devil – and free those who were held in slavery all their lives by the fear of death"* (Hebrews 2:14-15). These people were superstitious. They were enslaved by evil, and they were afraid.

For a while I sat talking with the *basibuku* (*headmen*) of the settlement, discussing my plans for the evening. We would begin by showing the Jesus Film and then I would share a Biblical presentation of the good news of the Gospel.

It was agreed that the plan was good and that we would begin as soon as darkness came. But first I had been summoned for an audience with the area tribal chief. He had heard troubling rumors regarding my ministry for which he must have an answer before I would be free to continue.

I did my best to match the pace of the *bagwasye basimwami* (messengers of the chief) as they clipped off the distance to the nearby kraal of the chief. In typical Tonga fashion, they set a walking tempo that would cause an Olympic speed walker to roll his eyes, but every once in a while I would jog a couple of steps while they weren't watching, just to keep things respectable.

Arriving at the chief's kraal, I was invited to take a seat, and after the exchange of a few BaTonga conversational niceties, I finally caught my breath. The old chief then cut to the chase. He described how he had heard troubling things about the ministry of the Baptist missionary. The word being rumored throughout the bush was that in the places where I had established churches, the people were being taught "*to drink blood*" and "*to eat human flesh.*" Such cannibalistic "*witchcraft*" could not be tolerated in decent BaTonga society.

After a thorough explanation of the Biblical doctrine of the Lord's Supper, and a gospel presentation based on the realities of the great symbolic truths represented in that sacred ordinance, the chief was at last convinced that I was not teaching practices of cannibalism. He agreed to be present for the evangelistic service that evening. *"I need to hear more about this Jesus of whom you keep on speaking."*

I left him seated there in the center of his kraal, only half-dressed and still answering questions from his headmen. I was surprised then, when the old chief, 20 years my senior, arrived only a couple of minutes after I got back to Sitali. *"He must know a shortcut. Or, could it be that unbelievable BaTonga pace? Um, I wonder if they've ever considered Olympic competition."*

That night was everything I had prayed it would be. After the Jesus Film and a well-defined Biblical message detailing the truths of the cross and resurrection of Jesus Christ, more than fifty men plus women and children made public professions of faith in the Savior. From subsequent later visits I can assure you almost the entire village was transformed that night.

Following the service, I made my way back down the hill to the boat where I would be sleeping. After using my flashlight to carefully search for crocodiles lying near and around the boat, I did my best impersonation of a triple long jumper, and touching the ground only twice in the final 15 feet separating me from the boat, I leaped to the safety of the 21rst century.

Snuggling deeply into the comfort of my trusty Jack Wolfskin sleeping bag, and tucking the near transparent security of my olive drab mosquito net between myself and the deck of the boat, I looked up into the unspeakable beauty of the spangled African night sky. In the distance I heard the jake brake grunting of a big male hippo and the howl of a jackal with its haunting wail sounding like an infant with a falsetto alto voice crying out in the night. In the tranquility of the moment I found myself naturally drawn to the habitual serenity of a conversation with my Father which customarily ends my day.

"Lord, I watched as You took the fight into the fortress of the evil one tonight. You marched into his stronghold and you set his captives free. You swallowed up death through the victory of Christ's resurrection and deliverance. You conquered the power of sin through the power of Your redemption. You destroyed the bondage of fear through the liberation of your promises. You devoured the devourer and made his empire a smorgasbord of faith. Lord, I got off this boat a few hours ago as an alien, a stranger, as a foreigner from half-way around the world. But tonight as I lie down to rest I sleep as a welcomed guest in the home of new brothers and sisters in Christ. It is only and always because of You. You, Oh God, are like nobody else! You are the great Warrior-God who subjugates the evil one. 'The thief comes to steal and kill and destroy. But You have come that these may have life and have it in abundance."

My mind could not help but wander back to the events of the week before. As I gazed into the black night sky, I recalled the ominous depth of the darkness at the end of that gun barrel and the threatening look in the eyes of the thief. Five armed men with hearts captured and controlled by the adversary had been his tool for discouragement and defeat in our lives. But that night at *Sitali*, fifty-two men plus women and children who had been *"held in slavery all their lives by the fear of death"* had been transformed and set free. That's a ratio in God's favor of more than ten to one!

A smile came across my face before sleep came. I marveled in amazement that an unlikely kid from Alabama would grow up to find himself one day in a place like this. It all seemed so natural to me at the time. I thought, *"This is why I was born. This is what the Lord planned for my life from the beginning."* I knew in that moment I was exactly where I was intended to be.

As I peered still deeper into the darkness, there in the stars of the night I imagined I could see a twinkle in the eye of God. And in my mind's eye I thought I even detected a smile of pleasure on His face. After all, for eons of time He had been planning all of this. He had planned to bring salvation and deliverance to this remote village of people in the Zambezi River Valley. Long before this time, He had put my life on a collision course with the lives of these people from one of the most inaccessible places in the world. That's why when I thought about it that night I had to join the Father in His smile. The robbery, the pain, our defeat and subsequent emotional trauma, the desire to go deeper and further with the gospel that had spawned in my heart from that experience – none of these things took Him by surprise. What He plans to do, He does do! That is the sovereignty of His purpose. If you look closely, you'll have to smile, too. He eats red dragons and ancient serpents for breakfast and he "swallows down" alpha predators for a midnight snack. He <u>loves to devour</u> the devourer. And what He loves to do, He does do. You can see that intentional look in His eyes!

SUMMARY: Part Two Life's Ultimate Adversary

The ancient Chinese warrior Sun Tzu taught his men to "*know your enemy*" before going into battle. For if "*you know your enemy and know yourself,*" he wrote, "*you need not fear the result of a hundred battles.*" But, Sun Tzu warned, "*If you know yourself but not the enemy, for every victory gained you will also suffer a defeat.*"[1]

The purpose of Part Two of this book has been to consider the nature and tactics of Satan in his intended destruction of our lives. He is our Ultimate Adversary. It is important for us to know him and his ways if we are going to be victorious over his devious schemes. We have seen:

- His position is one of perpetual opposition.
- His methods are accusation, deception, and intimidation.
- His occupation is constant surveillance – "a search and destroy mission."
- His goal is intentional annihilation.

Sun Tzu stressed the need to know both ourselves and our enemy if we are going to be victorious, but as believers we have one other consideration. In our spiritual battle for the survival of our souls, it is not enough merely to know the enemy and know ourselves in order to secure victory. We must be certain that we uniquely, intimately, and personally know God! That is the key to victory. That is the key to restoration. That is the key to our hope for the future. That is also the focus of the next section of this book.

PART THREE: What To Do When You're Not Victorious

TAYLOR

CHAPTER 7 Turning Maulings Into Monuments

"knowing that the same sufferings are being experienced by your brothers in the world. Now the God of all grace, Who called you to His eternal glory in Christ Jesus" (1 Peter 5:9b-10a)

I had just finished the last sip in my cup of Rooibos (red bush tea) when the young man made his way up the drive. He was walking with an obvious limp – not a seasoned limp like a man born with some long-endured impediment, but the fresh awkward gait of a man with a limp from a newly acquired wound.

As was often our practice, Shirley and I were visiting with our friends Buck and Rita De Vries. We were sitting with them on their front veranda in the cool of the late afternoon. Their porch was an especially relaxing place, the context of some of my fondest African memories. The natural stone work across the front of the house is surrounded with ferns and caladiums. The bright yellow and orange weaver birds in the nearby trees provide constant entertainment as they intricately design the mesh of their tidy and tight-fitting balloon-shaped nests using various pieces of roots, tendrils, and blades of grass.

Rita peered over the rim of her tea cup and moved her lips discreetly behind it as she whispered to Buck, asking the identity of the young man now approaching at the edge of the yard. Buck spoke quietly also, but the squint in his eye came from a troubled expression more than a strain to focus. His countenance was downcast like a man plagued with a lingering memory and it seemed to reveal an ache in his heart. The sight of this young man had somehow triggered a painful recollection in his mind. Finally he spoke, *"Ah, Ma, that is the young man who was recently taken by the crocodile there in Lake Kariba. He escaped with his life but his leg was injured very badly."*

Then I recalled the reason for the look on Buck's face – years before Buck and Rita had lost a son to a crocodile in Lake Kariba near the place where this young man had been attacked. The sight of this young man must have brought back some painful feelings for them.

As he neared the veranda, polite greetings were exchanged in all directions. The young man first spoke to Buck and Rita in Afrikaans, the Dutch-derived language of white South Africans. Then, after Shirley and I were introduced as friends from America, he spoke to us in English.

Initially the conversation was dominated by small-talk. The weather had been pleasant. The day was still. His family members were all fine. But then Buck injected intensity into the conversation. He asked him about his wounds.

At that, the young man took a deep breath and began to recite the events of that ill-fated day when his injuries had been acquired. He and a friend had been skin-diving in Lake Kariba, looking for small bright-colored exotic fish schooling among the bleached skeletal trunks and bare branches of dead trees. The trees had drowned many years before when the Zambezi River was dammed and the lake was formed. He described how after they had been diving a while, he had come to the surface only to be startled when he felt something bump into the back of his head. As he turned to see what had collided with him, he was shocked to see the snout of a massive Nile crocodile right in his face. He described his panic as *"irrepressible,"* and he feared initially that the giant reptile would swallow him head first. Instinctively, he brought his hands forward and pushed against the huge muzzle of the toothy creature now looming in his face. At the same time he turned and swam with all his strength to the nearest of the dead trees. Fortunately there was a low-hanging limb not very far from the surface of the water and with his last burst of effort he propelled himself out of the lake and grasped the branch.

Regrettably, the crocodile was close behind. The strength of the huge reptile's tail propelled the croc up out of the water and he fastened his teeth to the young man's left leg in the meaty part of his thigh just below his groin. Like a hungry man latching his teeth around a honey barbeque wing to strip the meat from the bone, the beast slashed the muscles from their moorings. As the weight of the huge crocodile pulled its body back into the water, the result was an enormous gaping tear that ripped down the young man's leg from his groin to his ankle. Bleeding profusely now and weakening quickly, he began to imagine what it would be like to be eaten alive by the colossal beast. As he hung there watching his blood flow into the water of Kariba and saw the eyes and nose of the crocodile protruding from beneath the surface, he admitted that he even started to cry. He was facing a hopeless situation. He knew as soon as he fell out of the tree the crocodile was waiting to devour him. As he prayed, he begged God to rescue him. And if not, he desperately hoped he would pass out before the feast began!

Fortunately, by this time his friend had surfaced also and was now back in their boat. Also, a couple of European fisherman who had been fishing for tiger fish not far away, had witnessed the scene and they, too, had made their way toward the young man. The arrival of the boats and commotion of the men had the effect of chasing the crocodile away, and the young man literally fell into the boat upon their arrival. After numerous surgeries, weeks in the hospital, and 287 stitches, the young man began to heal.

I listened closely as he spoke fervently and long while he told his story that late afternoon in Zimbabwe. But whenever he mentioned those scars I noticed he did not seem to speak of them with shame or embarrassment. Instead I detected what I thought was thanksgiving, gratitude, and pride in his voice.

By the end of his story a crowd of people had gathered from all around. A lot of them had questions. Many of them stared at the red and purple jaggedly serrated line running down the young man's leg, and shook their heads in disbelief. Some of the young boys who had come around were smiling and almost jealously exclaiming the

African equivalent of, *"Oh, Wow! This man was attacked by the great Sitale, and he lived to tell about it."* Buck's grandsons were there, too. They viewed the scars as a badge of honor rather than something over which to be ashamed. So, as I looked at that scar, I found myself asking, *"Is that really a scar, at all? Or had it somehow transformed into a badge of honor, and a testimony to adventure, survival, rescue, and the intervention of God?"*

Scars! We All Have Them

Amazingly, the Lord has a way of turning our spiritual maulings into monuments of His glory, as well. Does your life bear any scars from attacks by the Alpha Predator? Are you now ashamed of those scars or do you see them as monuments to God's grace – monuments to His working and intervention in your life?

The reason some people never recover from an attack by the Alpha Predator is because they are dominated with shame associated with the scars of that attack. When you are not victorious in your battle with life's ultimate adversary, the first thing you need to do is to reject the shame of the scars of your defeat and surrender those scars as platforms for monuments to the grace of God.

Please hear me. Be sure you understand what I am saying. Sin is shameful. We should be ashamed of our sin, but not perpetually ashamed. Once sin is genuinely confessed, forgiveness is granted, and grace is applied, the scars of our lives become platforms on which we build monuments to God's grace.

If you have dealt truthfully with your sin before God by honest and open confession, if you have received His pardon and His grace is in full operation in your life, then don't let the evil one destroy your joy by convincing you that you should live in perpetual shame. Even if you have failed in your fight against the devil, even if you have not been victorious in your response to the attack of the Alpha Predator, don't let him convince you that you are out of the race forever. Go to the Father in honest and forthright confession and then go on with your life. Don't live in perpetual shame.

Lysa TerKeurst says, *"Shame is the signature of Satan."*[1] Don't let the accuser keep you from serving Christ by overwhelming your heart with shame. Instead let God transform your shame into a platform of testimony for monuments of His overcoming grace.

Moses shamefully killed an Egyptian and hid his body in the sand, but do you really believe we will spend our eternity in heaven discussing Moses' shame? David shamefully took another man's wife and then killed her husband, but do you really think we will spend eternity in heaven focusing on David's shame? Peter shamefully and repeatedly denied Christ and swore he did not know Him, but do you really think we will spend eternity in heaven debating Peter's shame? No! Instead our discourse in heaven will be about the greatness of God's grace and the restoration of a murderer like Moses, the reinstatement of an adulterer like David, and the reestablishment of a denier like Peter. Our scars in heaven will not be the basis of shame but rather a platform for building a monument of praise to the glory and grace of God.

The promises of God are as sure for this world as for the world to come: *"I sought the Lord and He answered me and delivered me from all my fears. Those who look to Him are radiant with joy; their faces will never be ashamed"* (Psalm 34:4-5).

Shame is the first negative emotion ever recorded in the Word of God. We're told in the beginning that *"the man and his wife were both naked, and they felt no shame"* (Genesis 2:25). But after they sinned, they immediately sensed it and did everything they could to cover their shame. Mankind has been trying to cover shame's mark ever since. Only God can adequately deal with our shame.

TerKeurst continues by saying, *"I know firsthand how God can take what Satan meant for shame and use if for His glory. Think of it this way: Just when we think we've messed up so badly that our lives are nothing but heaps of ashes, God pours His Living Water over us and mixes the ashes into clay. He then takes the clay and molds it into a vessel of beauty. After He fills us with overflowing love, He can use us to pour His love into the hurting lives of others."*[2]

God takes our scars of shame and transforms them into platforms for monuments of His grace and His glory. Our scars are testimonies of how much we need Him and how dependent we are on Him for rescue and restoration. They are testimonies of hope for those engaged in the battle today.

Monuments of Priority

Our scars tell a lot about us as believers. What causes a person to suffer is one of the surest indications of what he or she believes in the most. The nature of a person's scars often reveal the priority of his convictions.

Take Job for example. He is a man who bore deep scars from multiple bouts with the Alpha Predator. But have you ever just stopped to closely examine his scars? What are the things that made him cry? What is the source of the deepest scars on his life?

Interestingly, we seldom hear him complaining about the sorts of things we might expect him to complain about. A lesser person might have focused on the pain of bereavement, or the overwhelming personal losses he had experienced, or the excruciating agony of physical disease. But Job focuses on these weighty and obvious sorrows only in passing.

What really bothers Job is what he perceives as the loss of his spiritual estate. The deepest scar of his experience is the loss of his sense of fellowship with God. He lost his consciousness of God's presence in his life. He lost his perception of spiritual peace. For him that was the one great crisis – the one great calamity in his life.[3]

As believers we would do well to ask ourselves what sorts of things cause us our greatest pain and suffering when we are not victorious in our battle against life's ultimate adversary. What sorts of things give us our deepest scars?

On the cross, what was it that caused Jesus His greatest pain? Was it the nails? No! Was it the crown of thorns?

No! Was it the pressure of the jagged wood against the lacerations on his back? No! As bad as these things were, His most desperate cry came when He lifted His head and cried out like a wounded animal, *"Eli, Eli, lema sabachthani?' That is, 'My God, My God, why have You forsaken Me?"* (Matthew 27:46). The greatest agony of the cross came from the absence of God in His life. Though He was totally victorious, sinless and unfailing, it was that lack of the Father's presence that gave Him His greatest scar.

If you want to turn your scars into monuments of God's grace, begin by asking what is it about your failure, your defeat, and your lack of victory in your battle against the evil one that really bothers you the most? Is it merely the personal embarrassment of your sin? Or is the deep scar of your heart caused by the interruption of your fellowship with God?

When John Chrysostom was arrested by the Roman Emperor, the ruler sought to make the great Christian recant, but without success. So, in frustration, the Emperor discussed with his advisers what could be done to the prisoner. *"Shall I put him in a dungeon?"* the Emperor asked.

"No." one of his counselors replied, *"For he will be glad to go. He longs for the quietness wherein he can delight in the mercies of his God."*

"Then he shall be executed!" said the Emperor.

"No," was the answer, *"for he will also be glad to die. He declares that in the event of death he will be in the presence of his Lord."*

"What shall we do then?" the ruler asked.

"There is only one thing that will give Chrysostom pain," the counselor said. *"To cause Chrysostom to suffer, make him sin. He is afraid of nothing except sin."*[4]

Is it that way in your life? Is that the nature of the scars in your life? Is your deepest concern about anything that will separate you from your precious fellowship with the Father? If you want to turn your scars into a monument to the grace of God, you must begin by examining the priority of your scars. What is it that really causes you to suffer? What is the source of your scars?

Monuments to the Prism of God's Grace

But not only are our scars monuments of God's grace because of their priorities. Our scars are also monuments of God's grace because of a prism. You may be wondering what I mean by that. But stay with me while I explain.

Peter tells us in this passage that our God is a God of *"all grace."* How much grace? *"All grace!"* The word used in the Greek for *"all"* means *"all without exception."* *"All"* in this sense conveys the idea of extensiveness and universality. When Moses met God in the burning bush experience of the Old Testament, God told Moses that His name is *"Yahweh"* or "I Am." Practically speaking God was saying to Moses, *"I Am . . . anything and everything you will need now and for all eternity!"* God is the Great Supplier of every needed grace, of every kind of grace, and of every means of grace. He tells us that *"His grace is sufficient,"* which means essentially that His grace is comprehensive and entirely sufficient for every need of any and every believer at any and every time.

Exactly one chapter before these verses, Peter describes God's grace as *"multi-colored grace."* The word in verse 10 of chapter 4 is *"poikilos."* In the HCSB Version of God's Word the word is translated as *"varied."* But literally the word is *"multi-colored."* Interestingly Peter uses the same adjective to describe trials that come into the lives of believers. In verse 6 of chapter 1 Peter says, *". . . though now for a short time you have had to be distressed by various trials. "* The word there is the same – *"multi-colored"* – multi-colored grace for multi-colored trials! Trouble and the grace to bear it come with the same inherent qualities. God's variegated grace is His provision for every "variegated need" in our lives. Our various trials reveal a prism of His grace. Thus our scars are transformed into monuments of God's grace.[5]

MULTI-COLORED GRACE

Multi-colored people with multi-colored pain
Chase multi-colored dreams with rainbows that refrain
Multi-colored broken hearts, all hope now dull and grey
With lifeless, muted, wash-out lives lost upon the way.

Their monochrome companions with broken crayons, too
Crave vivid colored sunsets but shadows they pursue.
They cannot find a palette wash to rinse their wounded
years.
The opus still evades them through the blinding of their
tears.

My canvas too was damaged; my sin had dulled the hue

TAYLOR

My failure had created a soul of solid blue.
But "Vibrant" came incarnate, colorful and bright,
Refurbished back a darkened heart with spectrums of His
light.

The Glowing Great Creator, the Artist of the skies
With colored, shaded, strokes of love – too splendid to
despise,
Put back a new creation that I had smeared and lost.
From crazy, clashing colors, He paid what it would cost

To take a fool's demolished work, and make it new again
And reinstate a work of art – the purpose of His pain.
His easel was a wooden cross, His canvas was a shroud.
The work of grace was His alone, and echoes through the
crowd.

The Love it takes to recreate a painting that was marred,
Is Love that shapes and now remakes the picture that was
scarred.
With newfound light and a brand new frame, the "portrait"
now is free.
For His multi-colored shades of grace have fully rescued
me!

– author.

Every pitfall or trial that comes our way is already covered by the multi-colored grace of God. He has a plan and provision for every situation we face. Every problem we encounter already has a divine solution. Regardless what multi-colored problems we may face, His multi-colored grace covers them all.

Monuments to the Purpose of God's Grace

The beginning of grace for each of us who believe is when God called us in Christ, but that beginning was connected with an end from the beginning, and the end is that He called us to His eternal glory. His *"eternal glory"* becomes the new goal of our lives.

For believers, therefore suffering takes on a different meaning and purpose than suffering in general – we suffer for our faith in Christ and we suffer that we might be conformed to His image. Thus our scars become a monument to God's purpose.

In verse 9, Peter uses a verb that is translated *"experienced,"* *". . . knowing that the same sufferings are being experienced by your brothers in the world."* Literally the word means, *"accomplished."* In the Greek, the word is *"epiteleo."* That little portion of the word, *"epi"* intensifies the meaning, in the sense of meaning *"fully"* + *"teleo"* which means *"to complete."* So the meaning behind the word is not just *"to bring something to an end,"* but *"to a determined goal."*

Originally the word referred to *"a turning point, or hinge in one's life at which one stage ends and another begins."* Later it came to mean *"the goal or the end."* Thus it conveys the idea of meaning *"to fully complete"* or *"to fully reach the intended goal,"* in the sense of successfully completing what has been begun.

The final meaning then is not just that sufferings will be brought to an end, but that these sufferings will completely fulfill their intended goal. Sufferings for the believer are neither purposeless nor fruitless – they have an intended goal. The Christian, therefore, awaits not the end of suffering but the goal of suffering.[6]

In this sense, scars define a purpose. The purpose is completion and thus an experience of extreme pain can become a "*hinge*" or "*turning point*" in our lives and is a vital step in the completion of the goal.

I love the way Martin Luther grasped this thought and described the Christian life and the challenges we must face along the way:

This life, therefore,
is not righteousness but growth in righteousness,
not health but healing,
not being but becoming,
not rest but exercise.
We are not yet what we shall be, but we are growing
toward it;
the process is not yet finished but it is going on.
This is not the end but it is the road;
all does not yet gleam in glory but all is being purified.[7]

J. R. Miller realized this and observed, "*Whole, unbruised, unbroken men are generally of little use to God.*"[8] A.W. Tozer recognized the same truth when he said that "*those whom God chooses to bless greatly, He must first wound deeply.*"[9] There is no blessing apart from the blows. There is no resurrection without the cross. There is no monument without the scars.

According to Scripture, God has called us ultimately to stand blameless before Him. The only guarantee that any believer will have a worthy report at the final judgment is God's faithfulness. Having begun this work in us, He will finish it. There is no possibility of failure or partial fulfillment. When God begins a work of salvation in a person, He finishes and perfects that work. The Bible says, *"He Who started a good work in you will carry it on to completion until the day of Christ Jesus"* (Phil. 1:6).

Most of us have lived long enough to realize that the painful experiences of life – those truly heart-rending, world-shaking, life-changing events of our past, have since become the hinges of significance upon which our lives have turned. I know that has been the case in my own life. God, Himself – the great *"God of all grace"* – has used those experiences to mold me, and make me, and refine me in His process of taking me, as a "messed-up" child, through His procedure of fashioning me into what He desires me to be.

Pain has a purpose. But in the end I find myself agreeing with Charles Spurgeon, that great old English preacher of many years ago, *"I bear willing witness that I owe more to the fire, the hammer and the file than to anything else in the Lord's workshop. I sometimes question whether I have ever learned anything except through the rod. When my schoolroom is darkened, I see the most."*[10]

After the attack of the Alpha Predator, if we are going to recover, we need to remember that pain has a purpose. And God is achieving His purpose in each of us today. Our scars become monuments to the purpose of God's grace.

Monuments to the Paradox of God's Grace

Our scars also are monuments to the paradox of His grace. The paradox is simply this: In contrast to the devil's intention, which is to disable, discourage, and destroy believers, God uses our suffering to bring about His gracious work in us and to prepare us to share in His eternal glory. In this way our scars are turned into monuments of God's grace.

The trials which are the means Satan employs for our destruction, God employs for our deliverance and development. Behind the problems of our lives stands the Alpha Predator seeking to devour us. But behind the Alpha Predator stands God determined to perfect and purify us, regardless of what Satan may try. God can take any tragedy or failure that explodes across our lives and use it to rain down reminders of the sweetness of His grace. He can take any scar and transform it into a monument.

Bob and Pam Parker are two of my favorite Zimbabwe missionaries. They and their family lived on the other side of Zimbabwe from where we lived in Kamativi, in the farming area of MaShonaland, in a town called Chinoyi. Chinoyi was known for its sugar cane farms, and it is a beautiful, verdant, green, rain-drenched part of the country.

Bob had asked me to come from Tongaland to help him with a pastor's training conference for the local pastors in his area. Because of the extremely rough roads in the Zambezi River Valley between Kamativi and the eastern side of Mashonaland, I opted to drive all the way around the country in a giant "horseshoe shaped" pattern – a trip of about fourteen hours. As the crow flies, the distance from

Kamativi to Chinoyi is much closer, but because of the rough roads in that deep bush country the time for driving that route is only slightly less, and going around would save a lot of wear and tear on the Land Cruiser and on my body.

One of the most predictable things about living in Zimbabwe is that sooner or later there is a shortage of almost every major essential commodity. During our years of living there, we experienced shortages with tea, bread, flour, fuel, dairy products, and a host of other things.

One of the worst shortages was the shortage of sugar. In fact, we were in the midst of a sugar shortage during the time I went over to Chinoyi to help Bob with his pastor's conference. There was no sugar to be found in all of Tongaland, so you can imagine my delight when I discovered a plentiful supply of that sweet substance upon my arrival in Chinoyi. I was so delighted with my discovery I decided to surprise Shirley and bring back two twenty kg packs of sugar. (Admittedly eighty-eight pounds of sugar is a bit of a confectionary overkill. But, it was one of those things that just seemed like a good idea at the time.)

On the morning I was scheduled to leave Chinoyi to make my return trip to Kamativi, I went by the local farmer's co-op and bought the sugar. I laid it carefully across the back seat of my truck and headed for home. I was so excited that I had found the sugar and that it was going to be such a big surprise for Shirley and the children.

By the time the week-long pastor's conference was over, I was missing the solitude of the deep bush of the Zambezi River Valley. Instead of going all the way around

Zimbabwe on the "good roads," I decided I would just take the shortcut home and go directly across the bush. It was a beautiful drive that day and I saw lots of wild game and wild country before the quick darkness of the valley began to set in.

As darkness came I was more determined to get home quickly, and since I had good lights on the Land Cruiser, I clipped along at a pretty good pace – at least a good pace for the roughed-out bush road I was traveling on that night. By the time I was in the Mola/Siakobvhu area, and I found myself delayed several times by the huge herds of Cape buffalo and elephants that often cross the road there. Because the long drive had frustrated me a bit, I was anxious to try and make up some time.

There is a straight stretch of road between Siakobvhu and Siabuwa, so I once again increased my speed. I was traveling along at a good "bush-cruising speed" when much too late I saw the road was completely washed out in front of me. Though I had time to touch the brakes, I didn't do any more than just engage the brake lights, and I hit the furrow that the torrents had cut across the road, at what can only be described as "full speed."

The Toyota shocks engaged immediately, and the springs responded more like a trampoline than a functional part of the vehicle's stability. Suddenly I was air born and the Toyota looked like the lead buggy in the Baja 500. Immediately everything not tied down in the vehicle flew up in the air and slammed into the ceiling. The eighty-eight pounds of sugar lying on the back seat was no exception. It catapulted against the roof of the Toyota, and the sacks literally disintegrated.

The result was much worse than you can imagine unless you've ever had more than eighty pounds of sugar explode down the back of your neck. Sugar dust seemed to rain down for an hour; though I'm sure I actually got the truck stopped and back up on the main road in only a matter of minutes. By that time, the biggest part of more than eighty pounds of pure white sugar covered everything in the vehicle.

Of course, those were the days when the mission agency for which I was working felt that air conditioning in bush vehicles was for sissies, and I was perspiring heavily in the hot and humid night of the Zambezi Valley. The sizable amount of the sweet stuff that found its way down the back of my collar made my shoulder blades feel like pancakes featured in an Aunt Jemima commercial, and my hair and beard began to form ultra-sticky sugar-coated stalactites.

A hundred miles from nowhere, I sat in the darkness of the deep bush night examining the damage by the dashboard lights and using my flashlight to scan the surrounding bush to make sure no hyenas were actually laughing at me! I could go on, but I think you get the picture.

After about four more hours of tacky discomfort, I finally made it home and began to explain to Shirley and the children why old dad was so late. By that time, even though I smelled like cotton candy and looked like a Yeti with a cake icing coiffure, they still welcomed me home. But when I explained that I had actually found plenty of sugar for the family before it had exploded all over the truck, it was not one of my more heroic moments.

I do think about that episode sometimes because it reminds me that even when things are exploding and falling apart all around us, God can take those explosions and rain down the sweetness of His mercy in our lives and cover our lives with the blessing of His clemency. That is the paradox of His grace. And it is one of the ways He turns our scars into monuments.

Are you walking with a limp? Do you have a broken wing? Do you bear deep ugly scars in your life? Have you been less than victorious in your battle with the Alpha Predator? What do you do now? Don't try to hide your scars! Use your damaged limb to point to God's redemption. Use your broken wing to demonstrate flight is possible only through the miracle of His enabling. Use your wounds as a tribute to the workings of His grace. Let God transform your maulings into monuments of His eternal glory!

CHAPTER 8 Reconstructing A Shattered Life!

"Now the God of all grace . . . will personally restore, establish, strengthen, and support you after you have suffered a little." (1 Peter 5:10)

"You'll never make it in a 'khombi,' Mufundisi." Baba Tuwe shook his head and bit his lip hesitantly as he spoke to me. He was looking at the vehicle I had been assigned to drive. I was a newly appointed missionary then and the "khombi" was my "temporarily allocated" vehicle "until something in four-wheel-drive could be found."

"Khombi" is the word used in Southern Africa to describe a mini-bus or van – usually a Volkswagen or Toyota. A "khombi" looks a lot like it sounds, and it is pronounced, *"comb-bee."* Yuk!

I must admit the "khombi" does have a rather interesting history. When I was a teenager, though it wasn't called by the same name in America, the "khombi" was actually the vehicle of choice for the hippie generation. During those years I had deliberately tried to distinguish myself from that particular counter-culture group by driving a muscle

153

car, but now I was driving a "khombi." Except for the absence of the psychedelic peace signs and colorful pastel flowers painted on the side, I could have fit in at Woodstock.

I was thirty years old then, I had been in Africa only for a few weeks, and I was doing my best to portray the persona of an experienced African adventurer. It was all going well, too, until they assigned me that "khombi."

For weeks prior to our departure from the states I had carefully selected just the right khaki shorts, roll-up sleeve safari shirts and hiking boots. I had even sent to Denver for a replica safari hat resembling the one Stewart Granger wore in *King Solomon's Mines*. I was actually beginning to look the part. Then . . . they assigned me the "khombi!"

In the months leading up to that moment, whenever I had daydreamed about how it would be to live "the true African experience," I had envisioned driving down a deep bush road in a vintage Land Rover, high-lift jack strapped to the back, evaporative canvas water bags hanging from the side-view mirrors, with ambient music from the soundtrack of *Hatari* being played in the background. But now, as I drove down the road in my "khombi," the only music score my mind could imagine was the old Scott McKenzie flower-power classic, *If You're Going to San Francisco – be sure to wear some flowers in your hair.* Just not good at all for the "intrepid bush missionary" image!

Now, Baba Tuwe was shaking his head and telling me the "khombi" would never make it to the location in the deep bush beyond Sanyati where his cousin lived and where I so desperately wanted to go. I'd have to make other plans.

After carefully considering our options and fully discussing the situation, Baba Tuwe and I concluded that the best plan would be to drive the "khombi" as far as I could to the edge of the deep bush, leave it there in the home village of another of Tuwe's relatives, and try to catch a ride with someone in something that could actually make it to the region beyond Sanyati.

The first leg of the journey went well. But it took a two full days of waiting before another vehicle passed by Tuwe's cousin's place. And, the vehicle that did finally come by was not a four-wheel-drive, but rather a dually dump truck that was taking supplies to a bush school in the faraway regions. *"Oh well, it would have to do."*

With three guys already in the front seat, Baba Tuwe squeezed in beside the others, while I opted to enjoy the great outdoors and a bit of solitude by crawling in the back of the truck. Mistake! Though it seemed like a good idea at the time, the result of that less-than-clever move was not exactly what I expected.

After hours of heavily perspiring while driving in the hot sun, mixed with a backdraft of dust coming into the box bed of the truck, I was completely covered with a thick sunbaked layer of hard clay. By the time we arrived at our destination, I had taken on the pottery-like appearance of a Navajo *Storyteller*. I had grit in my eyes and grit in my teeth and grit in bends of my arms and knees. I was filthy! And we still had to walk the remaining distance to the village.

We arrived at the settlement after dark. A bright-glowing fire was burning on the sand in the center of the village. After greetings from every person gathered there, I was invited to take a seat with the men at the fire. I was fascinated with their conversation, though at that time I understood very little of what was being said.

As I sat there, I was captivated with the sights and sounds of that remote and faraway place. I watched as the women walked silently away from the village carrying large clay pots on their heads, making their way to the river. Soon they returned with the pots obviously full of water. I could see small metal bowls used for dipping water from shallow pools, floating like small round canoes on top of their silt-colored content. They then set the pots at the edge of the fire until I began to see vapor traces illuminated from the light of the flames rise from the water. Next, using goatskins as potholders, they collected the pots and took them to a nearby hut. I thought to myself, *"They must be cooking something really special and something really big."*

At that moment the headman of the village spoke and jarred me out of my musing. He said, *"Come, Mufundisi."* I followed him to the hut and as he opened the door, I saw a sight I never dreamed I would see in the bush. A long metal tub full of steaming water set there in the center of the hut surrounded by burning candles. The headman smiled and then said, *"Mufundisi, your bath is ready."* As I slid down into the soothing soak, two young men guaranteed me privacy by standing outside the door guarding the hut. Like chocolate dropping off a Dairy Queen dip-cone on a hot Texas night, the thick layers of caked grunge began to peel off. In all my life I have never felt as clean as that night after that bath in the bush!

It was that night I fell in love with the deep bush African people – the most courteous, most hospitable, most cultured people I've ever known! It has been my experience that they are willing to do almost anything, and will go to almost any amount of trouble, to meet a need in the life of their guests. Many times since that night I have been the object of their extreme kindness.

But the point of my story is simply this; when you're dirty – I mean, really dirty – there is nothing that can satisfy like a good cleansing bath. When you find yourself as filthy as I was that night, nothing can bring a sense of restoration and well-being like that feeling of being truly clean once again. And that truth applies to your spiritual life as well.

You'll recall in the introduction to this book I stated that this book deals with *"How to Be Victorious over Life's Ultimate Adversary, and What to Do When You're Not."* This section of the book deals with the last part of that purpose – *"What to Do When You're Not Victorious."*

Have you ever felt you have failed so miserably in your response to the attack of the Alpha Predator that you just didn't think you could ever be clean again? Maybe that's where you are right now. Have you flopped in some foolish filth in ways you never imagined you could? Do you wonder if it can ever be the way it was before or if you can ever really make a come-back? Do you find yourself pondering whether a restoring decontamination is even possible and if there is any hope of rejuvenation or repair? Do you find yourself craving a clean start with God?

Louise Fletcher Tarkington expressed that sentiment when she wrote:

I wish there were some wonderful place
Called the Land of Beginning Again,
Where all our mistakes and all our heartaches
And all of our selfish grief
Could be dropped like a shabby old coat by the door
And never be put on again.[1]

Peter fully understood that yearning. His life had been mauled by the dual claws of sin and disgrace. He had experienced a sensation of hollow spiritual nausea when the Alpha Predator had grabbed him by the throat with the fangs of shame, indignity, humiliation and fear. He knew what it is to be confident – perhaps overconfident – in his spiritual walk, only to fail enormously and completely. And he had failed in ways he never thought he could. He had been so sure it could never happen to him. But then, it did!

Have you ever felt like that? Have you ever felt you needed a second chance, or a "do over" in life? Have you found yourself craving the cleansing of a radical restoration only the Father can provide? Do you find yourself longing for a reconstruction of your shattered life? Then Peter has a word of hope for you. *"Now the God of all grace . . . will personally restore, establish, strengthen, and support you after you have suffered a little"* (1 Peter 5:10).

Restoration is possible, but the great <u>hope</u> of restoration is not found in the possibility of it. Rather it is found in the certainty of it. The assurance of restoration can be traced to the certainty of its *Source*. The inspired promise of this verse is *"God, Himself, <u>will</u> . . . restore you!"*

The "Getting Up" Is Not Up to You

In 1996, Paramount Pictures released a major motion picture based on the true events surrounding the story of the Man-Eaters of Tsavo, Kenya. The film was called *The Ghost and the Darkness*. William Goldman wrote the screenplay and Stephen Hopkins directed the film. Though parts of the story were fictionalized for the movie, the film also portrays actual events that occurred during the historic building of the Kenya - Uganda Railway in 1898. During the course of the construction of that railroad, two man-eating lions killed an estimated 135 people. The local people thought these two marauders were more than lions. In fact they came to believe they were demons and gave them those names, *"the Ghost"* and *"the Darkness."*

Val Kilmer played the part of the military engineer, Colonel John Henry Patterson, and Michael Douglas played the role of a dauntless big-game hunter named Remington. At one point in the film Patterson and Remington, along with a band of Massai warriors, go out to ambush the lions who are now "hold up" in a thick stand of bush and thorn jess not far from the bridge construction site. Unknown to everyone except Patterson himself, on the night before the big hunt, the Colonel exchanged rifles with the local British doctor at the clinic. The result of that fateful decision was when the time came for him to make a killing shot on one of the man-eaters, the unfamiliar rifle misfired and almost cost him his life.

In a dramatic scene Remington confronts Patterson and asks, *"What happened?"*

Patterson swallows hard and looks up sheepishly as he says, *"A misfire."*

Remington asks, *"First time?"*

Patterson responds awkwardly, *"I don't know."*

"What do you mean, 'I don't know?" Remington insists.

Samuel, the African work-foreman interjects, *"The rifle belongs to Doctor Hawthorne."*

At that point, Remington stares at Patterson with a strained look of disbelief, and says, *"You mean to tell me that you exchanged rifles? Let me get this straight. You went into battle with an unproven weapon?"*

The look on Patterson's face tells it all. He is absolutely humiliated, demoralized, and ashamed. The "gut-sick" look on his face reflects the total agony of the admission of his mistake.

After that conversation, the Massai leave in disgust only adding more shame to Patterson's humiliation. Remington then sighs with amazement, and says, *"They have a saying in prize fighting – 'everyone has a plan until he gets hit.' You just got hit. The getting up is up to you."*

From that moment, and for a time after that in the film, Patterson grows sullenly quiet and plunges into a bout of depression and despair. Finally one night after Remington has come up with another plan for ambushing the lions, the Colonel dares to speak once again. He turns to Remington and says, *"Have you ever failed at anything?"*

Remington smiles slightly and huffs, *"Uh, only at life!"*

Later that night Remington's new plan for ambushing the lions also falls through. This time all the railroad workers leave in fear. And now it is Remington's turn to feel ashamed. That development is just too much for him, and it has a staggering impact on his behavior. He stumbles over his words as he tries to relate how beautiful the bridge and the railway would have been. Finally after listening to Remington stammer for a while, Patterson speaks up and repeats his own words back to him, *"You've just been hit. The getting up is up to you."*[2]

When I first heard those words, I thought, *"That sounds really good – 'the getting up is up to you.'"* But when it comes to an attack by the Alpha Predator, that's not the way it works at all. Ultimately, the "getting up" is <u>not</u> up to you! When the believer sins, and fails his Lord, as soon as he recognizes his failure, he should come back to Christ with contrite confession and repentance. But restoration is not something he can produce for himself. That is something only the *"God of all grace"* can do.

The Lesson Peter Learned

Peter had learned that lesson very well. The devastating result of Peter's denial and failure left him reeling under its weight. He had convinced himself he would never be capable of such defeat. He had felt that such spiritual collapse was somehow beyond him. The other disciples might deny Christ and let Him down, but Peter had assured Christ he would never be guilty of that. Yet the unthinkable had become a reality in his life. When he recognized that reality, his guilt was suddenly eclipsed by his shame. Then came the overwhelming self-incrimination. *"How could such a thing ever have happened to me? How could I have ever lowered my guard in such a way as to allow the Predator's fatal blow? How is it that with one act of cowardice I not only betrayed my Lord, but also managed to betray myself?"*

After all, Peter had been the leader. He had been the spokesman for the disciples. He had been an eyewitness to the miracles. He had been vocal and critical of those who had turned away from Christ when they *"followed Him no more."* He had made one of the greatest statements of faith to be found in the Word of God. He had been a part of the inner circle. He had been a member of the Lord's executive committee.

"How could I have ever allowed this to take place in my life? This just wasn't supposed to happen to me! Now how can I make a comeback? How can I get a new start? Will this be a blemish on my record in heaven for all eternity? Will I bear in my life the mark of shame I now sense whenever I look into the eyes of my fellow disciples? My whole life has been shattered! How can it ever be restored?"

Then came the isolation – the unique loneliness of a man who felt he had lost everything, thus no longer having any reason to live. Novelist William Styron described that sense of desperation with these words, *"In depression . . . faith in deliverance, in ultimate restoration, is absent. The pain is unrelenting, and what makes the condition intolerable is the [assumption] that no remedy will come – not in a day, an hour, a month, or a minute. It is hopelessness even more than pain that crushes the soul."*[3]

Some of those of you reading this book have experienced that unique loneliness and sense of isolation.

The country song writer Kris Kristofferson caught the essence of that emotional devastation in the words of his old song "Sunday Morning Coming Down." In his song he describes a man whose life had been a failure and who now walks through the world totally isolated from all others around him. Not long ago, when I heard the words, it reminded me of how Peter must have felt.

> *In the park I saw a daddy,*
> *With a laughin' little girl who he was swingin'.*
> *And I stopped beside a Sunday school,*
> *And listened to the song they were singin'.*
> *Then I headed back for home,*
> *And somewhere far away a lonely bell was ringin'.*
> *And it echoed through the canyons,*
> *Like the disappearing dreams of yesterday.*[4]

Peter felt the *"dreams of yesterday"* were rapidly *"disappearing"* now. He had failed so miserably and now he felt it could never be the same.

Self-imposed exile seemed to be Peter's solitary option for solace from disgrace, but the exile only amplified the volume of his own inner voice. The vicious cycle of self-imposed isolation and destructive self-incrimination drenched his mind with ever-increasing accusation until it spilled over with despair. *"It's hopeless! It can never be the same again."*

But then came the morning on the beach. There on the shore of the Sea of Galilee, Peter learned a lesson about restoration and renewal that he never forgot. John describes the lesson of Jesus' divine process of restoration in John, chapter 21. It is the lesson Peter describes in our present passage, and it is a lesson each of us needs to remember as well – especially when we find ourselves less than victorious in our battle with the Alpha Predator. *"Now the God of all grace . . . will personally restore, establish, strengthen, and support you after you have suffered a little."*

This is the lesson: it is the Lord, Himself, Who brings restoration to the defeated believer. And what makes this promise so significant is the use of a personal pronoun. Peter promises restoration, but more importantly he promises <u>personal</u> restoration by God Himself. In the original, the pronoun *"autos"* translated *"Himself"* is emphatically placed before four significant verbs that follow it in this passage. These verbs clearly emphasize God's personal interest in our restoration process. We are being personally restored by God Himself. It is a very <u>personal</u> process of restoration and repair. It is He, <u>Himself</u>, Who is doing it. He is intimately and personally involved in the suffering of our lives and our recovery from it.

Bruce Barton beautifully summarizes the great hope of this promise when he says, *"No matter what trouble you face, hard as it is, God has stamped your life 'temporarily out of order' with an emphasis on '*<u>*temporarily*</u>*.' A day is coming when the Great Repairman will . . . restore your life so that it works as God intended. You will be in mint condition, guaranteed to function as God designed."*[5]

ALPHA PREDATOR

After the Attack

During the years we lived in the Zambezi River Valley we had no television. The absence of that possession was a positive for our family. We spent free evenings reading to our children, interacting, and playing games. It was good for us all.

But here in America things have changed. The children are all married and are gone from home now, and Shirley and I once again have a television. In fact, typical of American television service, we have access to a selection from scores of channels and a variety of programs. Remarkably, for all the television watching I do, I could probably narrow that selection list down to three channels. I need a news channel – Fox News. I need a sports channel – I love college football in the fall and I always pull for the Crimson Tide. And I need the Animal Planet. To stay informed, I watch the news. To be entertained, I watch sports. But to relax, I watch the Animal Planet.

Among the many interesting programs I have seen on the Animal Planet is one called *After the Attack*. *After the Attack* tells stories of heroism and bravery as survivors of maiming, and sometimes deadly animal attacks, recount their tales. Dave Salmoni, the host of *After the Attack* and large predator expert, introduces viewers to the survivors of unique animal attacks as he helps these people work through the steps of their recovery process.

In the series, Salmoni recreates each critical detail of the attacks, trying to get a deeper understanding of what triggered the animal's hostility and how the victims survived. By the end of each dramatic episode, Salmoni and the survivors discover whether restoration is possible after the attack and how restoration can come into their lives.[6]

Spiritually speaking, I think this desperate position is exactly where many people are also. They want to know if there is life after failure, life after sin, life after an attack by the Alpha Predator. They want to know if there is any hope.

Peter's answer by inspiration and by experience is a resounding "*YES!*" "*Now the God of all grace . . . will personally restore, establish, strengthen, and support you after you have suffered a little.*" And he uses four graphic word pictures to describe exactly how the Lord goes about doing that. These four verbs describe the process by which God personally restores His fallen children.

Restored

Peter begins by saying, "*God Himself will personally "restore" you.*" The word translated "*restore*" is "*katartizo.*" That word "*katartizo*" is one of the most meaningful words to be found in Scripture. It means "*to fit or join together and so to mend or repair.*" It means "*to put something into its appropriate condition so it will function well.*" It means "*setting right what has gone wrong*" – "*to restore to a former condition as in mending broken nets.*"

What a wonderful word picture! God promises to repair the damage that sin and suffering have done. Even after gross failure on our part – after our lives have been ripped to shreds – it is His desire to make us what we ought to be.

Kenneth Wuest says this word carries the idea of *"equipping something or preparing it for future use."* Westcott writes that the word carries with it the idea of *"supplying that which is defective and mending that which is faulty."* In secular Greek the word was used as a medical term to describe the setting of a broken bone or the putting back of a dislocated limb into its right place. Sometimes the word was even used to describe the repairing of and the refitting of a damaged ship.

Therefore, what we can understand about the Lord's restoration is this – He intends to restore the defeated believer to fullness and completion. Alexander Maclaren stresses that *"katartizo"* *"is employed here for that great work of Divine grace by which our defects are made good, the rents which sin has made mended, the tarnished purity given back, the scars effaced. [All grace] answers the deepest of our needs. . . . When we think of our own defects and see how much is lacking in our characters, we may well feel nothing can ever fill these. Then the confidence of this brave text may hearten us. It is the God of all grace to Whom we look for our perfecting. No emptiness can be so vast and so empty that 'all grace' cannot fill it. No man has gone so far from the right way, or had his nature so lacerated by sin's cruel fangs, that 'all grace' cannot heal and repair the damage."*[7] God will not allow the work He began in us to fall short of His perfecting grace.

Established

The word translated *"establish"* is *"sterizo."* It means *"to make firm or solid."* And the basic idea is that of stabilizing something by providing a support or buttress from the outside. Through the process of restoration, God promises to give believers needed stability in order to make them solid and immovable. Thus they are given support and resolve to resist the onslaughts of the adversary. It is like the support Moses received from Aaron and Hur in Exodus 17 when they supported the arms of Moses by lifting them up on each side.

This buttress is the picture Peter is communicating concerning our ravaged lives. God stabilizes us with support that is dependable and secure. What is that support? In his next epistle Peter reminds believers that they have been stabilized by the truth. In fact, in 2 Peter 1:12, he tells them they *"are established in the truth."* We are established by the Word of God. Strong faith is a result of knowing all that God has revealed, and it has a firm foundation in sound doctrine and Biblical theology.[8]

Strengthened

The Greek word translated *"strengthened"* is *"sthenoo."* This is the only place we find this word used in the entire New Testament, and it means *"to cause someone or something to be or become more able or capable."* It carries with it the idea of being *"tempered."*[9]

No one really knows what his faith means to him until it has been tried in the furnace of affliction. There is something doubly precious about a faith that has come victoriously through pain and sorrow and disappointment. It is through suffering that God strengthens a man. We are hardened and solidified and toughened through suffering like fired and tempered glass or steel. Tempered glass is about four times stronger than regular or "non-tempered" glass of the same size and thickness. That's what the fire of trial or affliction does in our lives.

Supported

This word literally means "*to lay a foundation or provide with a foundation*" or "*to ground securely or to cause to be firm and unwavering.*" Whereas the previous word translated "*established*" refers to supports put around something to prop it up, this word refers to the secure foundation upon which something rests – literally, "*that which lies beneath.*" God's restoration gives us grounds for unshakable confidence and moving ahead with the Lord.[10]

When the true believer is not victorious in his battle with the Alpha Predator, his failure drives him to the bedrock of his faith. The agony of his defeat motivates him to determine what is superficial in life and what is really necessary. He is driven to the one thing upon which he can really build his life. Through God's restoration process the believer discovers that the one thing is really one person - Jesus Christ alone.

While I am writing these words, Texas, as well as other parts of the southwest United States is enduring a severe time of drought. Because of the deep dehydration of the earth, the foundations of the homes of many people throughout the state have begun to settle in ways never before experienced. Foundation repair companies have been called in to address these issues.

I was speaking with a friend last week who described the process being used to make the needed repairs on his home. He explained the best solution being offered by the companies is for them to come in and drill holes beneath the foundation of the house. *"They first lift the house from its foundation on huge jacks. Then they drill all the way down to the bedrock. Next, they pour solid concrete columns down to the bedrock. When these are firm and solid, they lower the house back onto these columns and the entire structure is supported soundly on the bedrock in this way."*

The bedrock of the believer's life is Jesus Christ alone. He is the firm foundation that never fails. It is the wise man who builds his life on this Rock. It is only that life that survives the storm! (Matthew 7:24 – 25)

Reconstructing a Shattered Life

"It's bound to be football! I excelled in football and the acorn doesn't fall far from the tree!"

"What acorn and what tree?"

We were home from the mission field and we were living in Albuquerque, New Mexico, at the time. Shirley and I had decided that our son Rye should be involved in some form of competitive sports, and we were having a discussion about the specific sport in which he should be participating.

It didn't take me long to figure it out. I had played football all during my growing up years. It was bound to be football! I was certain of it. We tried football. But football just wasn't Rye's game. (*Um? He must have had an off-day that day*.) Then we tried basketball, but basketball wasn't his game either. (*That's funny! Basketball was my second favorite sport*.) To make a long story short, baseball didn't work for him either. Nor did soccer! Nor did field hockey! Nor did volleyball! (The list goes on and I was beginning to wonder.)

Needless to say, it took me a bit by surprise when I came home one day and Shirley informed me that she had enrolled Rye on the local YMCA swim team. "*Swimming! That's one of the craziest ideas I've ever heard. I hate swimming! I was never any good at it. How could he possibly be any good at something in which I have so little interest?*"

Wouldn't you know it? By mid-summer Rye was recognized as one of the top three backstroke swimmers for his age group in the state of New Mexico. With every new blue ribbon, Shirley kept saying something about "*woman's intuition*." I kept mumbling something about, "*It must have just been a lucky guess*." But "*lucky guess*" or not, <u>swimming was Rye's sport!</u>

By the end of the season, his record had actually qualified him to be invited to compete in the State Invitational Championship Swim Match. And by that time, I was completely into it. I never missed a match. And the big championship day was coming soon. We were all excited.

Of course, I wanted to be a good "father-coach," but this wasn't football, and since I knew nothing about the skills or the techniques of swimming, I decided the best I could do as a "coach" would be to approach the whole "coaching" situation from a motivational perspective. I gave lots of "pep-talks" with words of encouragement and inspiration. With my limited exposure to swimming this seemed to make much more sense than making an attempt at advice regarding technique. I thought to myself, it would be kind of a *"win one for the Flipper"* approach. (Sorry! I couldn't resist it.)

I decided to include in this approach the use of two pointed object lessons. First, I bought a tee-shirt for Rye and had the words *"The Only Difference Is in the Heart"* printed on it. I emphasized to him that regardless of how well his competitors were coached or how talented they might be, the edge in competition always goes to the person who wants to win the most and whose heart is the most deeply committed to that goal.

Next, after digging through a storage box, I found an old MVP trophy that I had won in high school while playing football and that I had buried years before when we left for Africa. I decided to give it to Rye and to tell him to look at it from time to time during the days leading up to the big swim match and to imagine how nice it would be to win a trophy of his own. (The trophy was one of those gaudy three-tiered, fake-marble creations with a shiny golden character holding a football standing on top.)

When I gave it to Rye, I cautioned him to be careful with such a magnificent *"trans-generational athletic heirloom"* because *"if anything ever happened to it, it would be impossible to replace."* The exaggerated importance I attached to it and the embellished *hoopla* with which I described it had the desired effect. Rye responded with the typical *"ooh's and aah's"* of a nine-year-old. I realized even as I gave it to him, any real meaning or importance connected with the trophy had actually been attached to the long-since surpassed and fading athletic prowess of a small-town "has-been."

Now, I don't know if your experience confirms it or not, but I am convinced if you really want something to be "destroyed in seconds" just give it to a nine-year-old boy and tell him to be careful with it. Sure enough, not many days passed until Rye had the trophy broken into pieces. I discovered that fact one night when I walked down the hall and glanced in the half-open doorway of Rye's room. I shook my head with an *"I knew it"* sentiment as I glanced in his room and saw him sitting in the middle of his bed holding the broken trophy in his hands. At first I responded with disappointment as I thought, *"How could he dare treat such an outstanding gridiron treasure with such disregard and lack of respect?"* But then I felt the tug of God's Holy Spirit stirring in my conscience. And though I don't recall the exact words He used as He spoke to my heart, the gist of what He communicated was something like this; *"Why don't you get over yourself, let go of your foolish pride, and learn the lesson I'm trying to get across to you tonight?"*

With that, I stopped in the shadows of the hallway to watch more closely and to see what was happening. It was then that I saw the tears rolling down Rye's cheeks. In his little boy hands he was holding a roll of cellophane tape and was doing his best to repair the mess he had made out of the trophy. Of course, the more he awkwardly wrapped it with that sticky, tangling tape, the bigger the mess he was making out of the trophy. He slowly shook his head in frustration and hopelessness as he realized he would never be able to mend it on his own. I found myself identifying with that feeling.

I quietly turned and walked on to my room and got down on my knees beside my bed. It was one of those spontaneous prayer moments – not because I had planned to pray, but because I could do nothing else at the time but pray. *"Lord, so many times I've made such a shattered mess out of my life and I confess to You I've often made things worse by trying to fix them on my own. The consequences of my tragically inadequate solutions have taught me how useless it is for me to try to solve my problems all alone. I know I can't make it right when things go wrong. I can't solve the chaos created by my own sin. I need Your intervention and Your restoration in my life! I am wholly dependent on You. You, alone can restore and rejuvenate. You, alone can set all things right and make all things new. Your solutions emanate the distinct aroma of fresh air and clean rain, while mine always seem to reek with the odor of a far country and a pig pen. Please forgive me Lord, and restore me, and let me start all over once again . . . ."*

It would be wonderful if we were victorious in every encounter with the Alpha Predator, but that's just not the way it usually works in real life. In fact, this section of this book deals with what we can do when we are not victorious over life's ultimate adversary. In the previous chapter we saw when we are not victorious we need to let God turn our mauling into a monument of His grace. In this chapter we have seen that we need to let Him reconstruct our shattered lives with the personal restoration and cleansing that He, alone, can give.

That, after all, is the promise of God's Word. *"Now the God of all grace . . . will personally restore . . . you!"* (1 Peter 5:10). The great news of this verse is that God is on a personal mission to prove His point. And His point is that there is life after failure – there is life after sin. This is a point that not even the Alpha Predator can dispute. And it can all be summed up in the one word theme of this chapter describing the great hope and longing of every believer who has ever failed – RESTORATION! We all long for the reconstruction of our shattered life. There is no greater hope or aspiration for the defeated child of God. In the words of Ray Ortland, *"In heaven we will not be damaged goods. We will not carry psychological scars. We will be happy and whole!"*[11]

TAYLOR

CHAPTER 9 The Divine Dominator

"To Him be the dominion forever. Amen." (1 Peter 5:11)

The nun's face was ashen white and I saw a look of terror in her eyes as I glanced back over my shoulder. The two of us were flying as passengers above the Zambezi River Valley in a small classic African bush plane, a high-wing Cessna 180B tail dragger.   Our pilot, a young Missionary Aviation Fellowship recruit, was at the controls.

The pilot had picked me up earlier that morning at the Sesami airstrip and we had flown west, all the way to Hwange National Park. During our return trip back down the river we made brief stops at the villages of Mlibizi and Binga, so it was already late afternoon by the time we buzzed the crude tree-lined runway at Bumi Hills to chase the elephants and zebra off the primitive landing strip.   A Catholic nun who had been vacationing at the Bumi Hills Resort was waiting there to catch a ride back to the capital city. She took her seat in the back of the plane and I was seated in the off-side front seat across from the pilot.

While the pilot checked his flight plans, the nun and I exchanged polite greetings and small talk. I had just discovered she was an American when our conversation was cut short by the sound of the engine as it came to life. Since we had no headphones, the roar of the engine wiped out all other sound, and our conversation was completely stifled. All I could do during the flight was nod at her occasionally, smile, and acknowledge her presence.

Still, apart from the deafening engine noise, the flight back to Sesami was an enjoyable trip. We saw huge herds of elephants, buffalo, impala, and snowy white egrets, standing out in the sharp contrast of a reverse silhouette against the black pods of hippo in the shallows of the river. Seated as I was in a balcony seat often occupied by angels, I was mesmerized with my bird's eye view overlooking one of the wildest areas left in Africa. I found myself lost in thought as I gazed on the vast rough country below.

Suddenly the pilot spoke and brought me back to reality. I strained to hear him, but from what I could make out and from my limited ability to read his lips, I thought I detected the word "*pilot*." He seemed to be asking me a question. I assumed he was asking me if I wanted to "*pilot*" the plane. That was something I had never done before, and in that remote part of the world I thought it would be simple enough, so I nodded my head in affirmation to his question and reached forward for the controls.

Suddenly as I grasped the yoke, I could not remember whether pushing the controls forward or pulling them back would make the plane ascend. However, since I did not want to appear to be an "inexperienced novice," I decided to do whatever I did with enthusiasm. So, I confidently smiled and vigorously pushed the controls forward.

Mistake! Instantly the nose of the plane took a dive from the sky like a hunting falcon plunging in pursuit of its prey. At once, my view through the whirling prop, changed from the blue of the sky to the green of the forest, and I heard the nun scream behind me as she desperately clutched her rosary.

Immediately, the pilot took the controls back from me, and he repeated his question once again. This time he spoke it loudly enough and clearly enough for me to understand without any confusion. In fact, I understood then what he had been asking from the beginning. He had not asked *"Do you want to pilot?"* but rather he had asked, *"Are you a pilot?"* Without delay I shook my head and answered, *"No!"* At the same time I mocked a grin and mouthed the word, *"SORRY!"* He nodded and seemingly let it go. Apparently he had experienced it all before.

The nun's reaction, on the other hand, was not the same. In fact, when I finally got up enough nerve to look back at her, the first thing I noticed was that the "nun-like" countenance of serenity was completely gone from her face. While she didn't have much to say, I saw she had indentions in the shape of prayer beads on both palms. I won't go into a great deal of detail about how the incident ended that day, but I will tell you from the look she gave me when I said *"goodbye"* as I got out of the plane at Sesami, I don't think my first piloting attempt did a lot to enhance ecumenical relations in that part of the world.

Who's Really in Control?

Still, as with most of my slip-ups, I did learn some important life lessons that day. The primary lesson of which is this – Life seldom asks us the question *"Do you want to pilot?"* Yet for some reason we assume that we should, or at least that we should try, even though we are totally unqualified for the task.

The real question of life with which each of us must come to grips sooner or later is simply this: *"Are you a pilot?"* In fact, even better stated, the question is *"Are you the pilot?"* *"Are you capable of being in control?"* The only wise, safe, and accurate answer is a solid *"no!"* We may want to pilot our own plane and we may make some rather feeble attempts at doing so, but the results are usually rather catastrophic. Nowhere is this more evident than when we encounter the Alpha Predator.

We are not "the pilot" and we are not capable of being in control of our lives. When the Alpha Predator attacks, we need to remember the words of 1 Peter 5:11, *"To Him be dominion forever. Amen."* If you and I try in our own strength to fight back against, or stand up to, the attack of the Alpha Predator we will quickly discover that what we are attempting to do is humanly impossible. When we face that attack we need to realize that we need "Someone" Who is far above ourselves to adequately handle the situation on our behalf. This is where the Lord, the Divine Dominator, Himself, comes in. He alone can meet the need, give us strength, and provide deliverance from the Attack of the Alpha Predator. And He alone can restore us when we fail.

The Apostle Peter ends his Alpha Predator passage with a verse highlighting the *"dominion"* of the Lord. If we are not careful, we may assume that the final verse, (verse 11) is nothing but a "wind down" benediction to an adventurous passage describing our ultimate adversary and our encounter with him. But actually, this final verse is the key to overcoming and surviving the Alpha Predator's attack. In this final section of the book I have dealt with what to do when we fail, when we fall on our faces, when the attack of the Alpha Predator overcomes us, when we are not victorious. This final verse is the key to recovery when we have yielded to failure and defeat.

In my "airplane parable" I shared above, you'll note when I lost control of the plane, there were three things I had to do in order to regain stability.

(1) First, I had to recognize there is a pilot and it is his job to pilot the plane.
(2) Second, I had to admit my inability, submitting and surrendering complete control to him.
(3) Finally I had to realize that there was someone by my side who could successfully fly the plane regardless of how badly I had flopped in my attempt at piloting and that I would be safe and secure as long as he was there beside me.

So what do we do when we've taken control of our own life but find our life is crashing?

Dominion

STEP NUMBER ONE: RECOGNIZE THE SOVEREIGNTY OF CHRIST.

He has *"dominion"* and He is sovereign over every area of life. He alone can keep the "plane" in our lives from crashing. He alone can restore us if and when it does.

The word *"dominion"* is a special term for power. This power is the power to rule or control. It conveys the idea of *force, strength, might,* and especially *manifested power*. It is a term of sovereignty. It is a characteristic of the God Who rules all the circumstances and situations of our lives. And it implies the domination, subjugation, and suppression of any and all enemies of those who have surrendered their lives to God.[1]

It is for that reason David, the wise warrior-king and *"a man after God's own heart,"* prays to God concerning those who had attacked him, *"God, knock the teeth out of their mouths; Lord, tear out the young lions' fangs"* (Psalm 58:6). He realizes he must surrender the situation into the hands of Someone else.

In Job 12:16, Job describes this *"dominion."* There we read, *"True wisdom and [dominion] are His, the misled and the misleader belong to Him."* When you find yourself *misled* by the ultimate adversary, when you are attacked by the Alpha Predator – the great *misleader*, it is important to recall that both the *misled* and the *misleader* are under the Lord's control. They both *belong* to Him.

The God Who Owns Me

Perhaps the best definition of *dominion* I've ever come across is this: *"The independent right of possession."*[2] Look closely at that definition. *"The independent right of possession"* means everything I am and everything I have belongs to God. That is His right. He owns me.

Years ago, the Lord brought a special friend into my life. Clark Henderson is one of the most gifted musicians and deeply committed Christians I have ever known. He wrote and sang a song that perfectly describes the concept of *dominion* Peter describes in this passage. During the years we worked together prior to my family's return to Africa, I asked him to sing that song so often, the words still remain in my heart today.

> *When the blood of young rams could no longer atone,*
> *For the harvest of sin that mankind had sown,*
> *God sent His Son for all who'd believe,*
> *And He sprinkled His blood on my heart's mercy seat.*
> Chorus:
> *I've been bought with a price I can never repay,*
> *From slave market of sin to a new life today.*
> *I'm no longer my own I won't get what I deserve.*
> *For the God Who owns me is the Lord Whom I serve.*[3]

As the great Pilot of the universe, God controls everything. His *dominion* is described in Isaiah 40:25-26. There the prophet records the voice of the Lord: "'*Who will you compare Me to, or Who is My equal?' asks the Holy One. 'Look up and see: who created these?' He brings out the starry host by number; He calls all of them by name. Because of His great power and [dominion] not one of them is missing.*"

The Lord is in charge of it all. And though there is a great Alpha Predator against whom we must be on guard, there is One greater still Who is both Alpha and Omega, the

Beginning and the End, and He is the One Who has dominion over everything. Nothing is too difficult for Him. No force of evil is so strong that he cannot conquer it. No broken heart is so shattered that he cannot mend it. No situation is ever hopeless. The Alpha Predator is never so powerful that the Lord cannot overpower him.

Who or What Can Dominate an Alpha Predator?

I have a confession to make. I genuinely struggled to come up with a mental picture for this final chapter. I needed an image foe the absolute dominion of Christ. In my mind I had a general concept of what I wanted to say. I had envisioned some sort of Super Apex Predator who could adequately represent the Lord. I had pictured something so overpowering and so phenomenal that Satan, the Roaring Lion, the Alpha Predator, would be so completely overshadowed by the magnitude of that Great Beast – that he would be utterly dwarfed in the light of His presence. I must admit most of the animals that came to my mind were the giant prehistoric ones.

At first, in my mind's eye I visualized the giant lizard king, a colossal Tyrannosaurus rex stepping out into a clearing where a lion was proudly roaring, only to see the lion spinelessly and furtively slink away. But then I felt my heart shouting, *"No, Bigger!" "Stronger!" "It needs to be something more impressive if it is to represent the Lord."*

Then I began to imagine the great megalodon. The megalodon was the largest shark that ever lived. It was a fifty-four foot-long whale-eating machine with a bite radius that was ten feet wide. It weighed as much as fifty-two tons, and it had the strongest bite force of any prehistoric predator; a whopping eighteen to twenty tons of pressure. It could have easily swallowed a tyrannosaur, and certainly it would have had no problem downing a lion in one gulp. Still, the symbol just didn't seem adequate. In fact, every hyper-carnivorous super apex predator I could conjure up somehow came up lacking.

Then it hit me! The Lord, Himself gave us the image I had been looking for, in Job 40 and 41. There we find the depiction of a God so breathtaking that He keeps megalodons in a fish bowl on His kitchen table. We find the portrait of a God Who amuses Himself with Tyrannosaurs like you and I frolic with Chihuahuas on our laps. At least, according to His Word, that is the way He deals with *leviathans* and *behemoths*! This is the picture I was looking for. This is the portrayal of a God Who has absolute <u>dominion</u> over everything regardless of its size or power.

Remarkably, God's answer to Job's devastating experience when he had been ravaged by the Alpha Predator was a revelation of the immensity of Himself. There is something steadying and renewing about a vision of how formidable God really is. There is comfort in the reality of His dominion in our lives. We must begin by recognizing that dominion.

Surrender and Submission

<u>STEP NUMBER TWO</u>: FIND FREEDOM THROUGH FULL SURRENDER TO CHRIST'S DOMINION.

The restoration experience of Job ends with these words, *"I know You can do anything . . . Surely I spoke about things I did not understand, things too wonderful for me to know . . . I had heard rumors about You, but now my eyes have seen You. Therefore I take back [my words] and repent in dust and ashes"* (Job 42:2-6).

The biblical book of Job ends with Job's posture of absolute surrender and submission and with recognition of God's dominion in his life. In light of the unlimited dominion of God, that's the only proper way for any restoration story to end.

Actually, I believe a case can be made from Scripture that all restoration stories end with surrender and submission to God's dominion! Check it out for yourself. Whether Jacob (Genesis 28), or David (Psalm 51), or Peter (John 21), or the Prodigal (Luke 15), all restoration stories end that way.

Unqualified Surrender

"Jump? What do you mean, 'jump?'"

I had arrived late at our rendezvous point. There are always delays in the deep bush of Africa! Whether it involves snakes to kill, or flats to change, or herds of elephants to maneuver around, there always seems to be something that causes a delay.

My guides were waiting patiently when I switched off the ignition, set the hand brake on the truck, and unbuckled the seat belt. The giant shade of the acacia tree would have to do for a shelter for the truck until I returned. The tree was at the end of the road where I parked that day. Another three hours would be required to walk the remaining distance to the remote village where I had promised to share the gospel over the next few days.

I swung the backpack up onto my shoulders, but felt the weight of it disappear before I could buckle the straps. The younger of the two African guides had taken it from my back and insisted on carrying it. *"It would not be polite for you to carry this burden, Mufundisi. It is the Tonga way."*

I barely got the door on the truck locked when they began to stride up the game trail that also served as a path to the village where I would be speaking that night. Africans usually begin a walk at the same pace they conclude it. "Full speed" seems to be the only pace they know when it comes to walking.

By the time we completed the first hour of the walk, the shadows of the bush had grown longer and longer, and now, it was completely dark. It was one of those rare nights at the end of the rainy season when clouds covered the sky. There was no light at all.

Normally, even if the moon is not shining in Africa, the stars are so bright there is enough light to walk safely merely by the glow of the stars. That night, however, was an exception to that usual standard. There was no light at all beneath the canopy of the trees in that part of the deep bushvelt.

Not to worry! The Africans have an uncanny ability to see in the darkness. They never even broke stride. I was now third in the procession and was keeping up literally by listening to the rhythm of their footfalls ahead of me. Not wanting to come across as a weak-eyed *Mukuwa* (Tonga word for *"white man"*), I was trying to think of some natural excuse for taking a break, at which time I planned to subtly retrieve the flashlight from my backpack.

Just as I was mulling over in my mind the plausible excuses for taking a breather, suddenly the steady beat of those footfalls came to a stop. *"You guys tired?"* I asked, trying to disguise my heavy breathing by pulling my lips tight across my teeth.

"No, Mufundisi. There is a river that crosses our path here. We are going to have to jump."

"Jump? What do you mean, 'jump?'"

The older of the two guides explained that because of the rains, the river was swollen and deep. Even though he had used the diminutive word for "river," which meant that it was really more like what we would call a creek back in the states, he went on to explain that the banks were high and steep. *"Fortunately,"* he said, *"it is not too wide."*

"How wide is this water?" I asked.

"Not very wide, Mufundisi. It is only a little river. Less than three meters!"

"Meters, meters, meters? Let me see now, one meter is thirty-nine inches, times three, divided by twelve. And it is a little less than that." My mind raced back to my college math days as I tried to quickly figure the distance that loomed before us. I estimated it was likely somewhere around eight or nine feet wide.

The guide spoke once again, *"Not too wide, Mufundisi. Even the young boys can jump it when they go out with the cattle each day."*

"Where do the cattle cross?" I asked.

"They cross just there a little further down, where the river is flat and wide, but there are crocodiles, Mufundisi."

"Crocodiles? Um . . . All righty then! Just let me get my flashlight and we'll jump this thing."

I reached into the pocket of my backpack where I always kept my flashlight and my heart sank. The extra batteries were there, but no flashlight. *"Oh no!"* I had left it on the floorboard under the seat after I had helped that old man get his *scotch-cart* (an African donkey wagon) out of the ditch the night before. I had no flashlight.

Standing there in the darkness I realized I was in what the Tongas might describe as a real *"mapickle."* I had no light. We were about to jump a three-meter wide creek, in pitch black darkness, and the crocodiles were waiting just downstream. *"OK guys, how are we going to do this?"*

The older of the two began to explain. *"We'll jump first since we have done this many times and we know how far it is to the other side. Then you jump. Take three steps backward, and then count your steps as you run toward the edge. On your third step jump, and we will catch you on the other side. That will keep you from running into the thorns with your eyes in case you jump too far."*

"Great!" I was already struggling with temporary night-blindness, now he was telling me I might make that condition permanent if I, or they, or both of us missed our assignments on this jump.

The younger guide laughed softly and with three quick steps propelled himself into the darkness and landed safely on the other side with a "feet-planting" thud. The older guide then said, *"See Mufundisi, it's easy. We'll catch you."* With that he turned and seemingly with no effort cleared the creek. *"OK, Mufundisi, we are ready. You can jump now."*

As I took three steps backward I kept my mind focused on the location where I had last heard his voice. Just before I took my first step I thought for a moment that I could see his teeth shining as he smiled on the other side. Then it was one, two, three, and I was airborne! I hung in the air for a moment as I reached out with my toes to feel the ground on the other side. And then there it was!

The Africans quickly wrapped their arms around me and stopped all forward motion. I landed safely, and with a real sense of relief we completed the remainder of our journey to the village. That jump taught me a great deal about full surrender.

Find Freedom through Full Surrender

Christ can regain control of our life even if our life is crashing. In fact, as remarkable as it sounds, He can regain control of our life not only if our life is "crashing," but even when it has already "crashed." However, there must be absolute surrender, and that involves a transparent heart confession and absolute submission to Him. We must be willing to take the leap! All of God's restoration stories end like that.

David gives us a good example of that kind of unqualified surrender and the restoration that follows it in Psalm 142. "*I cry aloud to the Lord; I plead aloud to the Lord for mercy. I pour out my complaint before Him; I reveal my trouble to Him. Although my spirit is weak within me, You know my way. Along this path I travel they have hidden a trap for me. Look to the right and see: no one stands up for me; there is no refuge for me; no one cares about me. I cry to You, Lord; I say, "You are my shelter, my portion in the land of the living." Listen to my cry for I am very weak. Rescue me from those who pursue me, for they are too strong for me. Free me from prison so that I can praise Your name. The righteous will gather around me because You deal generously with me"* (vv.1-7).

The first six verses of that psalm are an example of clear and unqualified surrender. The final verse is a pleading for, and a declaration of, full restoration. Look again at what David says. *"Free me from prison so that I can praise Your name."* It appears that David's ability to fully praise the Lord and his ability to be able to once again stand up to his full spiritual height is dependent on the Lord setting him *"free from prison."* There is a sense in which a believer can fully and freely praise the Lord only when he is set free from the prison that confines his heart. This is what David is experiencing here. His context is incarcerating him. He has been chained by the circumstances of his surroundings. He needs a comeback!

This is a Biblical principle that can be uniquely understood by the believer who has failed his Master and who has been defeated by the Alpha Predator. While clearly it is a prison of his own making, it is nonetheless a prison that is real and restraining. It is a prison that restricts the freedom of praise. His greatest need is to be set free. He cannot set himself free, so he must come to the place of full surrender to Christ's dominion.

Escaping Mental Afterimages

"Afterimages" are those spots of light we see after gazing at the sun, after experiencing a photo flash, or after staring at approaching headlights on the highway at night. The image lingers long after the experience. Scientifically speaking, it involves fatigue within the photoreceptors of our eyes and the desensitization of the cells of our retinas and our body's response to it.

Some scenes from the experiences of our lives leave an indelible imprint on the surface of our memories. Try as we may, we can't forget them. They are like mental "afterimages," present with us continually, memory reflections that will not go away. Some scenes from our past are so impressive, so vivid, and so graphic that they stay in our minds long after we have seen them with our eyes.

I once saw an eagle that had that effect on me. I was scheduled to show the *Jesus Film* and to bring a gospel message one night at a place called Chipale. Chipale is a typical deep bush village located far off the beaten path in the far inland south central side of the Zambezi River Valley. I had brought a group of volunteers with me and had deliberately arrived early in order to have time to invite people from that area to the film and worship service that evening.

Upon my arrival that day, I discovered they were having a football tournament at the local soccer field. People and teams from all the surrounding villages had gathered for the big match. I decided this would be a great opportunity to invite many people for the activities of the evening, so I made my way to the grassless, dusty, field where hundreds of people had gathered to watch the game.

In many ways attending one of those village football matches is very much like going to a football game in the states. Invariably in those villages there will always be some players who are truly outstanding athletes, and I have come across some of them who, I am sure, if having been given a chance, could have "made it" as star players anywhere in the world.

Also, invariably at those big matches there will always be attention seekers who, like rainbow heads and body painters at American football games, seek to bring attention to themselves in all kinds of bizarre and curious ways. One young man that day made himself obnoxious by walking around the field monotonously blowing a homemade "vuvuzela" in everyone's ear. It was like those used during the World Cup Soccer matches in Johannesburg, South Africa. Another highly intoxicated man gathered a crowd with his loud, slurred philosophical verbosity and his self-convinced pretense. In fact, he pretended to be an expert on every subject relating to soccer and life. He kind of reminded me of the guy I always seem to get seated next to on a long international flight.

People are people pretty much wherever you interact with them. There are certain characters in every crowd. Faces change. Cultures change. But, people don't. I thought I had seen it all.

But then I saw the man with the eagle. Obviously he had caught the eagle in a trap or after it had been injured or caught in a snare. He had bound its legs in such a way as to prevent adequate flight for escape. Now, after the final winning score by his favorite local team, the man standing on the sidelines released the eagle from his grip and it flew as best it could to the center of the field where unable as it was to land and perch on its bound legs, it "crashed" and pathetically tumbled in the dirt. At this point the players and their supporters ran toward the helpless creature, encircling it as a mass of screaming, cheering fans. The eagle was obviously terrified and frantically flapped its wings in an effort to flee, but the people just surrounded it laughing, jeering, and scornfully mocking its inability to take flight.

I'll never forget the look in the eyes of that eagle. That look is an afterimage that remains today. Anger, bewilderment, terror, shock, disorientation and hopelessness! With its crest ruffled, mouth gaping, and eyes darting in every direction looking for a way out of its humiliation, the once proud sky creature, now disgraced with captivity, was the essence of shame.

After a while the people grew tired of their mockery and turned their attention to other things. In the meantime the poor bird was left along and some young boys began to take pity on it and made repeated efforts to approach it and set it free. But each time they came near, the huge raptor would strike at them with its sharp beak and try desperately to escape. It would beat its wings against the dust, and cause all kinds of commotion in an effort to get away. In fact, it did almost everything it could do except for the one thing it needed to do to gain its freedom. It refused to surrender so the boys could untie its legs.

I have a feeling there are those reading these words right now who somewhere along the way have seen the same look as I saw in the eyes of that eagle that day. Perhaps you have seen it in the mirror each morning as you have looked into your own eyes. The Alpha Predator somehow surrounded you, attacked you, defeated you, and humiliated you and now you find yourself living with that defeat, conquered by shame. The afterimage of some failure, some defeat, some foolish sin still burns in your mind and the desperate prayer of your despairing heart has become, *"Father free me from prison so I can praise Your name."* Your situation has overwhelmed you, and you find yourself searching desperately for a way of escape. But that freedom will never come until you take step two and find that freedom through full surrender to Christ's "independent right of possession" of every dimension of your life.

The Restorative Presence of Christ

STEP NUMBER THREE: FIND HOPE IN THE REALITY OF CHRIST'S RESTORATIVE PRESENCE IN YOUR LIFE.

"And remember, I am with you always . . ."

I first met Tom Elliff in 1981 when he and I were being appointed as new missionaries to Zimbabwe, Africa. During those early days of missionary orientation, in preparation for our departure, and then in subsequent years of ministering and serving together, the Lord blessed us with a unique and precious friendship. It is a friendship for which I will be eternally grateful. Tom Elliff is the most extraordinary man I have ever known.

Shortly after our arrival in Zimbabwe, Tom and I were both craving adventure and an opportunity to be a part of "cutting-edge" missions. After talking with Dr. Rob

Garrison, a medical doctor from Sanyati who traveled occasionally up into southern peripheries of the land of the Tongas, we made plans to accompany him to a place called Syamchembu.

Tom and I had thoroughly discussed the upcoming trip, and we decided we wanted to be "good" new missionaries. Since neither of us had ever been a missionary before, we didn't know exactly what that meant – to be "good" new missionaries – but as best as we could determine that meant we were committed to get along on this trip by eating what the people ate and basically by living as they lived.

Anyway, we left home devoted to be as "indigenous" as possible, and to survive and enjoy the trip like genuine sons of the bush. Things went really well – at first! We sampled lots of Tonga dishes without any adverse effects, learned much about the local tribal ways, killed a snake or two, and had a wonderful time ministering with the Tonga people. Everything was going just dandy.

Then, we were offered a goat's head! (We found out later that while it had been cooked, the goat's head had been left setting in the sunshine for three days after it had been cooked. So, by the time we got it, it was a bit rank, to say the least.)

I was the first one to get sick, and I have to tell you, there is no comfortable place to be sick in a bush village. The lack of facilities and the lack of privacy make it a miserable place to be ill. The next morning, trying to find some relief from the nausea, I confined myself to lying on the floor of a tent, while contemplating whether or not I was going to die.

As I lay there with eyes closed, drifting in and out of fitful sleep, imagining I was going to have to get better to die, I suddenly felt a strange presence in the tent with me. As I opened my eyes, there, six inches from the end of my nose I saw the head of a big African cobra. I thought to myself . . . *Oh No; I really am going to die!* In an effort to clear my head, I blinked my eyes and opened them widely once again. The snake was still there. This was no dream or fevered hallucination. It was really there, and it was really in my face. *"Um. This kind of takes the sparkle off the whole 'indigenous' routine."*

(I have to admit a short fleshly thought did skip across my mind. I thought at least it will look better for the state denominational paper headlines back home to read, *Rookie Missionary Bitten to Death by Huge Cobra in the African Bush* instead of *Rookie Missionary Barfs Himself to Death in the Bush.* I was so sick.)

But then I began to focus my eyes up the long slender body of that cobra. When I did so, I saw a hand holding the cobra by the tail. Beside that hand was the smiling face of my friend Tom Elliff. (By this time he, too, had gotten sick and had killed this thing on one of his frequent trips to the bush. Now he thought it would be a hilarious prank to dangle it in my face while I slept in the tent.) He laughed and said, *"Don't worry, friend. I've already killed it. It can't strike you now."* He clearly enjoyed the gag much more than I did at the time.

Well, to make a long story short, our friendship survived a major test that day, but as always, I also learned an important lesson of life. Sometimes when a person is defeated by the Alpha Predator, the shame of that event is all he can focus on anymore. In fact, when he concentrates on his failure, it gets right up in his face and that's all he can comprehend – no tomorrow, no future, no recovery, and no restoration – only failure and defeat! The shame of his defeat at that point becomes crushing. His heart is shattered by his shame, and his shame, like a cruel Satanic "shapeshifter" transforms itself into hopelessness.

But if by faith he will focus his gaze beyond the Satanic intimidation of that hopelessness, he will find the Hand of One Who has seized that hopelessness by the tail, and the smiling face of a Friend Who looking down from heaven, says, *"And remember, I am with you always, to the end of the age!" "To Him be the dominion forever. Amen."* Find hope in Christ's restorative presence in your life. He is the Pilot. He controls everything. He is the Divine Dominator. He is there for you. He is there to rescue your crashing life.

CONCLUSION Finding A Place To Stand

"I have written briefly, encouraging you and testifying that this is the true grace of God. Take your stand in it!" (1 Peter 5:12)

REALITY DISCLAIMER – *Adventure is always more fun telling about it later than it is living through it at the time.*

Right now, I know some of you are going through the "miserable" phase of an Alpha Predator attack. Satan has attacked and you have failed. He has laid a trap and you have been defeated. He has pounced and you are crushed. You desperately need to find some answers and a cure for your shattered heart. You urgently need to hear a fellow struggler say to you, *"It's going to be all right. I've been there. I got through it. God will bring you through. There is hope beyond where you are right now."* <u>That really is the purpose of this book</u>. I've written to remind you there is hope beyond today. There is peace beyond your heartbreak. There is restoration beyond your failure.

But when you can't see tomorrow, how do you live through today? When you can't envision a future, how do you get by right now? When you can no longer sense the pleasure of His fellowship, how do you survive the agony of your interim? Between the time of your failure and the time of your restoration, where do you stand in the meantime?

In the final verses of his first epistle, Peter gives a vital answer to those questions. After he pens 1 Peter 5:8 -11, the great "Alpha Predator" passage which has served as the Scriptural basis for this book, he concludes his writing in verse 12 with these words, *"I have written briefly, encouraging you and testifying that this is the true grace of God. Take your stand in it!"* Peter is saying, during the period of pain that exists between your ruin and your renewal, you must *"take your stand . . . in the true grace of God."*

Standing Knee-deep in a Swamp on a Dark African Night

The fabric of my khaki safari shirt turned a dark tobacco brown as I knelt on one knee and the water rose across my chest just at the height of my arm pits. I was hunting lechwe in the Lochinvar area of the vast Kafue floodplains at the edge of Lake Manyeke in south-central Zambia. Hunting lechwe is unlike any other hunting I've ever done. The fact that it is done on the floodplains means much of it is done while wading in water ranging in depth from three inches to three feet. The floodplains are generally as flat as a table top so most shots are taken at extreme ranges; some more than a quarter mile.

The Kafue lechwe is the largest of three sub-species of lechwe found in Zambia; the other two being the red and the black lechwe. They are mid-size African antelope similar in appearance to the well-known impala, only slightly larger and with a greater aquatic, water-loving disposition. Lechwe have a water-repellant greasy substance on their legs that makes it easy for them to run in knee-deep water. They use that to their advantage against the approach of predators. The herds are usually made up of animals of the same sex, except during mating season. Sometimes the groups can be composed of hundreds of individuals. All males have horns, so choosing the "right" animal based on its horn length is a lot like choosing the tallest tree in a forest when you're standing at its base.

But, since this was to be my last lechwe for the season I was waiting for a special and superb animal before I took a shot. Now the sun was sinking low, and I was running out of time. Champion, my national parks-provided guide, was there at my side as he had been faithfully all day long.

When I first saw the big ram he was more than five hundred yards away and was lagging a short distance behind the others in the herd. From the size of his massively fluted lyre-shaped horns, it was easy to tell even at that distance he was bigger than any of the others in the group. His mahogany brown coat with its black tips on his face and legs was shining brilliantly in the refracted light of the sunset. I found myself tempted to delay the shot in order to enjoy the beauty of the moment. But this ram represented food for my family for the next few weeks, so after closing as much distance as possible, I carefully slid my finger into the trigger-guard of the .257 Weatherby Magnum and knelt in the waist-deep water as I readied myself for the shot. With Champion kneeling near me in the water, I took one last deep breath, rested the stock of my rifle in the cradle of the inner tube-bound shooting sticks, settled the crosshairs of the Leupold on the antelope's shoulder, released the safety, and squeezed the trigger.

What happened next took me by surprise. Though I had previously shot many lechwe on the floodplains of the Kafue, and even though I had become accustomed to sloshing through water in the pursuit of that task, I had never before taken a shot from a place where the water was so deep. With the water now surrounding my chest, the rifle barrel was parallel to the water and only about six inches above it when the bullet ignited. The 100 grain Nosler ballistic tip projectile sped to its target at more than 3500 feet per second. The force of the muzzle blast and percussion shock of the bullet's explosion had an incredible impact on the surface on the floodplain. The water split open like a mini-version of the scene from Charlton Heston's Red Sea crossing, and the sound was phenomenal. Fortunately for me, the big lechwe dropped in his tracks.

As any experienced hunter knows, hunting is fun until you shoot something. Then the work begins. With the rifle held above my head, Champion and I made our way in the water to where the animal fell, and we began to size up the situation. It didn't take long to realize we had a problem. We had begun our hunt in the early afternoon and by now we were miles away from the truck. There was no way we could drag the animal through the water for the entire distance back to the truck. Somehow we would have to get the truck closer, and by now it was getting dark.

We considered our options. The only flashlight we had with us was the small mini-mag light secured in one of the bullet loops above my shirt pocket. One of us would have to go for the truck with the light, while the other one would have to stay behind with the ram, standing in waist-deep water in a dark African swamp while waiting for the first to return. I hate it when it is my time to be "the other one!" But as I thought it through, I knew I had to stay. I had taken the animal, and I was responsible for it. Besides, Champion knew where there was a group of African fisherman camped by the lake. He would go by on his way to the truck and collect them. They would be invaluable help when it came to loading the lechwe in the truck.

With the last remaining light, Champion and I waded around in the water looking for a "high" place where I could stand and wait for his return. Finally Champion put his foot down firmly in a solid place just a few feet from the lechwe carcass. He said, *"This is your place to stand!"* Africans have an uncanny ability to "know things." That spot turned out to be the highest spot in the area. And though the water there still came up to just below my knees, it turned out to be the best place in that area of the marsh to take a stand. At least it would be far better than waiting in waist-deep water.

I watched as Champion and the flashlight faded into the darkness. In the distance I could hear some zebras barking. I find that sound to be one of the most enjoyable sounds of the bush. It's unique to say the least. In fact, it is like no other sound I've ever heard. I'm not sure I can accurately describe it, but I've heard it so many times in the bush I will never forget it. It's a bit like the braying of a donkey mixed with the shrill yipping sound of a lonely puppy. I always recognize it immediately even when it originates at a distance, and to me it is one of the true sounds of Africa. Now, the sound was coming closer. Finally, the trotting herd passed by me so closely, they actually splashed water on my face as they passed.

Over the years I spent in Africa I conditioned myself to enjoy solitude, so at first I enjoyed standing there in that immense, desolate place. Seldom in my life have I actually experienced loneliness. But there, in the silence of that vast, dark floodplain I felt very much alone. While I can't give you from experience an opinion on everything, I can give you an opinion on this – there is something unusually quiet and lonesome about standing alone in knee-deep water on a dark African night. It was quiet – intensely quiet – so quiet I could hear my own heart beating and the scratch of my beard against the cotton collar of my shirt whenever I looked around. And as time passed I begin to hear things moving in the water. I never knew what it was, and I was never able to determine how far away it was, but from the sounds of splashing water I could determine something was definitely there.

Forty-five minutes after Champion left I heard the first hippo bellow; then another, and still another. I could not determine exactly where they were, but I began to realize they must be coming out of the deeper water of the lake into the shallows of the floodplain to feed. *"Hey, I was in the shallows!"* A fleeting thought of the floodplain's close proximity to the lake also crossed my mind. *"Wait a minute, there are crocodiles in the lake. Um! The blood from the lechwe must be spreading through the water now. I wish I could remember what I read that time about how far crocodiles can smell blood in the water."*

Then it was silent again. Extreme silence has a way of intensifying the other senses. I began to see shapes in the darkness, and I began to smell the scent of animal dung floating on the surface of the giant liquid pasture in which I was standing. My sense of touch also seemed to be increasing. In fact, my legs began to "feel" strange. It was like a burning sensation mixed with the feeling of a small electrical current – kind of like the way the tip of your tongue feels when you're still stupid enough to test nine volt batteries that way. I was beginning to feel a bit uncomfortable. Later, when I got to the light, I found out seven blood-sucking leeches had attached themselves to my calves. (This would be a good place to insert the above "reality disclaimer.")

At last, I saw the bobbing twin lights of the Toyota coming across the flats. Champion and the others were on their way. Fortunately, we were actually able to get the truck close enough on patches of semi-dry land to load the lechwe and be on our way in only a matter of minutes. When I glanced at my watch, I realized I had been standing in the darkness for two hours. I'm just grateful to God that during the course of the whole ordeal I had *a "high" place to stand*!

True Grace not True Grit

Whenever you find yourself standing waist-deep in shame on a dark night of guilt following an Alpha Predator attack, your great need is to find a place to stand. The crucial nature of that need is that you find the right place to stand. Peter was fully aware of the pointlessness of trying to stand up to a satanic attack in his own strength. That's the wrong place! He had failed miserably when he tried to stand up to the evil one's intimidation while being tempted to deny Christ. He had tried to just grit his teeth and stand in his own strength, but he learned a forever lesson from his failure – the need of his life was not true grit but rather true grace.

That being the case, grace had come to mean everything to Peter. In fact, the word "grace" is used in every chapter of his first epistle. Peter knew that apart from grace he didn't have a prayer. He could never forget that terrible night by the enemy's campfire when his life had been ransacked by the Alpha Predator's attack. But neither did he ever forget that morning on the beach when Christ's grace had fully restored him. He learned what you and I must learn, as well. God's grace is universally sufficient for every need of any and every believer at any and every time in his life. God already has a solution for any problem we may ever face and any failure we may experience. His grace is one hundred percent sufficient!

Sufficient grace is the truth revealed powerfully in the words of the prophet Micah when he said of our great God of all grace, *"Who is a God like You, removing iniquity and passing over rebellion for the remnant of His inheritance? He does not hold on to His anger forever, because He delights in faithful love. He will again have compassion on us; He will vanquish our iniquities. You will cast all our sins into the depths of the sea.*" (Micah 7:18-19) And, that's why Peter stresses his very purpose in writing his first epistle was to "*encourage*" fellow believers to "*take a stand . . . in the true grace of God.*"

Reinstatement

One of the ancient Greek historians used the word that is here translated, "*encourage*" to describe the reinstatement of a Greek regiment that had lost heart and was utterly dejected. The general of that regiment sent a leader to talk to his men, to "*encourage*" them and to rally their hearts. The result of that "*encouragement*" was that courage was reborn and a body of dispirited men became fit again for heroic action.[1]

That allegory describes the restoration experience that had taken place in Peter's life. And that is also the restoration experience God wants to take place in the lives of each of us who have disappointed Him. You see, because of his experience, Peter uniquely understood the great truth of the concept of grace. Each of us who have failed must also come to understand it. This is the great truth – **God's purpose is to redeem and restore from ruin those who have failed, yet who still belong to Him**. His is a grace of redemption – a grace of renewal – a grace of restoration – a grace of beginning again! The Alpha Predator does not win – end of story! Peter wrote his epistle to *"testify"* to that truth. I have written this book to *"testify"* to that truth. *"This is the true grace of God."* This is your place to stand! *"Take your stand in it!*

ABOUT AUTHOR
Steven R. Taylor

The locals call it "**Khaki Fever**" – a term often used by safari guides in Zimbabwe to describe the condition of a person who falls hopelessly and helplessly in love with Africa. Symptoms include extreme infatuation and fascination with the land, the people, and the wild animals of that faraway place. I have had a severe case of "khaki fever" for as long as I can remember! From my earliest recollections I have been drawn to the people, the wildlife, and the countryside of Africa, and for the past thirty-plus years my life has been bound up in one way or another with all things relating to that captivating continent.

It came as no surprise, then, to those who knew me well, that in 1981 after graduating from Samford University and Southwestern Baptist Theological Seminary, and after serving for a few years as pastor of churches in Texas and Alabama, my life took a radical change of direction. It was then, in response to the call of God, my wife, my family, and I pulled up the roots of our American way of life and moved to Zimbabwe, Africa, where we served for years as international missionaries. One would think that such a radical move would help assuage the intensity of my "khaki fever," but all of those years of living in the deep bush of

Zimbabwe Africa did nothing to alleviate the fervor of my love and addiction. In fact, if anything, those years merely increased my passion. Even now, every year I return with a group of intrepid volunteers to the remote Zambezi River Valley in order to spend time with the wonderful BaTonga people who live in that region. In my case I fear the condition is incurable!

Seldom do things in the course of an adult lifetime work out so that childhood dreams actually come true. However, the Lord has blessed me uniquely. I have been privileged not only to live out my life in obedience to the divine call of God, but also to experience abundant opportunities for authentic adventure. I was favored to live in a time when I personally experienced the last generation of "real" Africa before the waves of western society washed across its face and eroded the wild raw beauty of an indigenous civilization that is now almost gone. Thirty years ago I knew a timeless people who lived simple lives, carried spears and knobkerries for protection against wild animals, and sometimes even wore bones in their noses. They communicated with drums and swift runners carrying messages from tribal chiefs. Now, those same people have adult children who communicate with cell phones and ride in comfort-equipped buses from bush villages to growth point communities where they regularly check their e-mail accounts.

I'm back in the states these days, living with my wife Shirley and pastoring a church in the Panhandle of Texas. We have three grown children, all faithfully serving the Lord, and four wonderful grandchildren.

"Khaki fever" still burns deep in my soul. Indelible

memories of an action-packed past are forever seared into my way of thinking. Treasured recollections from those wonderful years in Africa are splattered across my mind like mud spots on a land cruiser after an adventurous afternoon in the bush. Should I wash the truck? I don't think so. Instead I think I will just pass it on to those who may come after me who choose to travel the same rough roads.

TAYLOR

NOTES

Introduction

[1] http://www.news.bbc.co.uk/2/hi/uk_news/409714.

[2] www.aidantrust.org, The Wild Goose, from volume 7, Number 4, Spring 2001.

Chapter 1

[1] 1Peter 5:8 Commentary
http://www.preceptaustin.org/1peter_58-14.htm #Be on alert (1127).

[2] Common Pickpocket Techniques
http://www.corporatetravelsafety.com/safety.tip/category/pickpockets/tip/common-   pickpocket-techniques-the basics of pickpockets.

[3] http://www.sermoncentral.com/sermons/breaking-free-from-the-past-brian-bill-sermon-on-forgiveness-for-others-57501.asp.

[4] Vincent, Marvin Richardson, Vincent's Word Studies in the New Testament, (New York Charles Scribner's Sons, 1905) Volume One – Commentary on Mark 13:34-37 – gregoreuo.

Chapter 2

[1] Haresnape, Geoffrey, <u>The Great Hunters</u>, (Cape Town; New York: Purnell Publishers, 1974) Section: Great Escapes – Harry Wolhutter – Introductory notes.

[2] http://www.wikihow.com/Survive-a-Lion-Attack - various.

[3] Capstick, Peter Hathaway, <u>Death in the Long Grass</u>, (New York: St. Martin's Press, 1977) pp. 9 -10.

[4] http://www.preceptaustin.org/1_peter_59.htm # Resist - anthistemi (436).

[5] http://en.wikipedia.org/wiki/8-track_tape.

[6] Ravenhill, Leonard, <u>Why Revival Tarries</u> (Minneapolis, MN: Bethany House Publishers, 1959) Chapter 20 - Known in Hell.

[7] Earley, Dave and Gutierrez, Ben, <u>Ministry Is</u>, (Nashville, TN: B&H Publishing Group, 2010) Chapter 34 – Giving Hell a Headache, pp. 34-41.

[8] Studd, C. T. quoted by Norman P. Grubb, <u>C. T. Studd: Cricketeer and Pioneer</u>, (Fort Washington, PA: Christian Literature Crusade, 1985), p.13.

Chapter 3

[1] Gaddis, Mike, <u>First Light</u>, "Sporting Classics Magazine," (Columbia, SC, LiveOak Press, January – February 2011) pp. 28-32.

[2] http://www.preceptaustin.org/1_peter_59.htm - # Brethren - adelphotes (81).

Chapter 4

[1] Bulpin, T. V., The Hunter is Death, (Long Beach, CA: Safari Press, 1987)

[2] http://preceptaustin.org/1_peter_58-14.htm - # antidikos (476)

[3] Vincent, Marvin Richardson, Vincent's Word Studies in the New Testament, (New York Charles Scribner's Sons, 1905)

[4] http://preceptaustin.org/1_peter_58-14.htm - # diabolos (1228)

[5] DeCaprice, Jesse, Remember the Duck – short story – http://www.bibliofaction.com/read/ViewStory.aspx?story=d85469c6-7bb7-48b2-bbac-bc987e1b5ab7

[6] http://www.preaching.com/sermon-illustrations/11548498/page-2/ - Bill Klem story.

Chapter 5

[1] Pease, Sir Alfred, The Book of the Lion, (New York: Charles Scribner's Sons, 1914) pp. 166-167.

[2] Thomas, Kevin, Night of the Lioness, http://www.africahunting.com/content/2-night-lioness-338/

[3] http://www.encyclo.co.uk/define/Digitigrade

4

http://en.wikipedia.org/wiki/Animals_Are_Beautiful_Peopl
e, 1974

5

http://www.ecotravel.co.za/Guides/Wildlife/Vertebrates/M
ammals/Big_5/Lion/african-lion-hunting-habits.htm

6 http://bible.org/illustration/consumed-their-own-lust

7 Ogilvie, Lloyd John, Facing the Future Without Fear,
(Ann Arbor MI: Servant Publishing, 1999)

8 http://en.wikipedia.org/wiki/The_Princess_Diaries_(film)

9

http://www.worldinvisible.com/library/hudsontaylor/hudso
ntaylorv2/hudsontaylorv212.htm

10 http://www.medicalnewstoday.com/articles/41339.php

Chapter 6

1 http://www.goodreads.com/author/quotes/58.Frank_
Herbert

2 http://preceptaustin.org/1_peter_58-14.htm - # (2212)
zeteo - seeking.

3

http://animals.nationalgeographic.com/animals/mammals/hi
ppopotamus/

4 http://preceptaustin.org/1_peter_58-14.htm - # (2666)
katapino.

5 Ibid.

[6] http://en.wikipedia.org/wiki/Deep_Impact_(film)
[7] http://preceptaustin.org/1_peter_58-14.htm - # (2666)
katapino.

Summary – Part Two
[1] http://www.goodreads.com/author/quotes/1771.Sun_Tzu

Chapter 7

[1] TerKeurst, Lysa, Who Holds the Key to Your Heart?
(Chicago, IL: A Focus on the Family Book, Moody
Publishers, 2002) p. 5.

[2] Terkeurst, Ibid. p. 7.

[3] Mason, Mike, The Gospel According to Job, Chapter –
The Loss of Peace, (Wheaton, IL: Crossway Books, 1994)

[4]

http://www.lmworldwide.org/uploadedFiles/OBR/Teaching
_and_Study_Resources2/Practical_Ill_sample_pages.pdf

[5] http://www.preceptaustin.org/1_peter_410-13.htm - #
(4164) - poikilos – manifold.

[6] http://www.preceptaustin.org/1_peter_59.htm - # (2005) -
epiteleo – accomplished.

[7] Luther, Martin,
http://www.goodreads.com/quotes/22880-this-life-
therefore-is-not-righteousness-but-growth-in-righteousness

[8] Billheimer, Paul E., Don't Waste Your Sorrows, (Ft.
Washington PA: CLC Publications, 1977) p. 69.

[9] Tozer, A. W., The Root of Righteousness, (Camp Hill, PA: Wingspread Publishers, 1986) p. 157.

[10] Charles Haddon Spurgeon, *Spurgeon's Sermon Notes*, ed. David Otis Fuller (Grand Rapids: Kregel, 1990), p. 307.

Chapter 8

[1] Tarkington, Louisa Fletcher, Our Paper, *The Land of Beginning Again*, (Concord Junction, MS: Massachusetts Reformatory, Volume 37, December 11, 1920) p. 597.

[2]

http://en.wikipedia.org/wiki/The_Ghost_and_the_Darkness

[3] http://thinkexist.com/quotation/in_depression---faith_in_deliverance-in_ultimate/331235.html

[4]

http://www.lyricsfreak.com/k/kris+kristofferson/sunday+morning+coming+down_20494870.html

[5] Barton, Bruce, The Life Application New Testament Commentary, (Wheaton, IL: Tyndale House Publishers, 2001) 1 Peter 5:10.

[6] http://animal.discovery.com/tv/after-the-attack/after-the-attack.html

[7] http://www.preceptaustin.org/1_peter_510-14.htm - # (2675) katartizo – perfect.

[8] http://www.preceptaustin.org/1_peter_510-14.htm - # (4741) sterizo – confirm.

[9] http://www.preceptaustin.org/1_peter_510-14.htm - # (4599) sthenoo – confirm.

[10] http://www.preceptaustin.org/1_peter_510-14.htm - # (2311) themelioo – establish.

[11] Ortlund, Ray, Sermon – How to Lose with God, http://www.preceptaustin.org/1_peter_510-14.htm

Chapter 9

[1] http://www.preceptaustin.org/1_peter_511-14.htm - # (2904) kratos – dominion.

[2]

http://machaut.uchicago.edu/?action=search&resource=Webster%27s&word=Dominion&quicksearch=on.

[3] Henderson, Clark D., "Bought With A Price" (Heart Song Music/AARB, 1983) Used by permission.

Conclusion

[1] http://www.preceptaustin.org/1_peter_511-14.htm - # (3870) - parakeleo – exhorting.